FULFILLING YOUR PURPOSE

COMPLETING YOUR LIFE'S ASSIGNMENT

SOLOMON OSOKO

FULFILLING YOUR PURPOSE:
Completing Your Life's Assignment

Copyright © 2015 by Solomon Osoko
All rights reserved.

The copyright laws of Switzerland protect this book.

No portion of this book may be copied or reprinted for commercial gain without the written permission of the author and publisher, with the exception of brief excerpts in articles, magazines or reviews.

The use of short quotation and occasional copying for personal or group study is permitted and encouraged.

Unless otherwise identified, all scripture quotations are from the King James Version of the Bible.

ISBN -13: 978-3-9524512-0-5

Published in Switzerland.

For further information, contact:

Solomon Osoko Ministries
www.solomonosoko.com
sales@solomonosoko.com

Solomon Osoko

CONTENTS

FORWARD 5
INTRODUCTION 6
   CHAPTER 1: BE READY FOR CHANGE 7
   CHAPTER 2: DISCOVERING AND DEVELOPING YOUR POTENTIALS 16
   CHAPTER 3: DISCOVERING AND FULFILLING YOUR DESTINY 29
   CHAPTER 4: DISCOVERING AND FULFILLING YOUR PURPOSE 38
   CHAPTER 5: LIVING FULFILLED 49
   CHAPTER 6: LIVING LARGE AS PRIESTS AND KINGS 58
   CHAPTER 7: KEYS TO SUCCESSFUL EXISTENCE 77
   APPENDIXES 84

FORWARD

Every man is created for a purpose.
Purpose, however, cannot be fulfilled until it is discovered.
This book will put you face to face with your destiny and help you to answer important questions about your life's purpose.

This little manual will go beyond helping you to locate your destiny to empowering you to fulfil your purpose.

While the pursuits of career, wealth, fame and material things of life may grant you success and temporary happiness, it cannot grant you fulfilment. Only the completion of your purpose gives you fulfilment in life. I detected that truth many years ago when I quit my job as an associate director of an international bank to pursue my calling as a Pastor. God has used that experience to energize my divine mandate to empower people towards fulfilling their destiny and purpose on earth.

The first book I wrote, **"Fulfilling Your Destiny"**, was published a decade ago and I have seen God use it to deliver many lives from frustration, defeat, failure and diverse molestations of the enemy.

I have to wait for another 10 years to write this completing part, **"Fulfilling Your Purpose"**.

This book is foremost, a product of divine revelations.

It is also a result of various "School of ministry" seminars, workshops, leadership training and Bible School teaching, we held in our Church for the past decade. It is a compendium of tested knowledge, practical experience and timeless wisdom of the Scripture.

Congratulations on investing in purchasing this unique book that will help you to fulfil your destiny and accomplish your purpose on earth.

This life manual will put you in control of your life and empower you to have dominion in your area of life's assignment.

It is however required that you practice what you learn in this book for it to profit you. Your faith without work is fake.

Congratulations. It is time to stop merely existing.
It is time to discover your destiny and live in your purpose.

Congratulations. It is your time to rise and shine.
It is time to step onto the stage of your life and do exploits.
Your life of purpose has just begun…

INTRODUCTION

Every man on earth is on a unique assignment. That emphasises the truth that you are God's idea, and you are on a mission in this world.
That explains why your gifts, skills and personality are unique.
God has created you purposefully to solve a unique problem on earth.
Your relevance, reward and fulfilment are found in fulfilling your assignment. Fulfilling your life assignment would demand co-operation from your side. You are solely responsible for discovering and fulfilling your life's assignment. You will need to discover, develop and deploy divine potentials (deposited in you) to accomplish your assignment.
This book has come to help you discover your purpose so that you can maximize your time on earth to accomplish it.

"Some people make things happen, some watch things happen, while others wonder what has happened" **Unanimous**

Which group do you belong to? At the end of this book, I hope you will join the group of those who make things happen in any area God has called you to add value to mankind.

This book will:

1. Switch you alive and help you to answer major questions of life, including, "Who am I? And what is my purpose on earth?"

2. Align your thought with that of your Maker (Rom. 12:2)

3. Align your path with the purpose of God for your life (Jer. 29:11)

4. Teach you, your "rights and responsibilities" as a creature of free will (Gal.6:5; 2 Cor.5:10; 2 Peter 1:10.)

5. Nudge you to develop your potential to perfection (Matthew 13:31)

6. Empower you to take charge of life as manager of God's resources

7. Prepare you to enjoy fulfilment in life by fulfilling your purpose

8. Help you to leave behind a legacy that will enrich the world than you met it.

CHAPTER 1: BE READY FOR CHANGE

The path of the righteous is like the morning sun, shining ever brighter till the full light of day. **Prov. 4:18 (NIV)**

But the path of the righteous is like the light of dawn, which shines brighter and brighter until full day. **Prov. 4:18 (ESV)**

Be ready for a change! There is always a better and higher level available for you in the Lord. The path of a believer is created to shine brighter every day as s/he follows God who leads such from glory to glory.

You are a fragile jar of clay filled with treasures.

Deposited in you are great potentials to enjoy a great existence.

All you need to do is to discover and maximize your potentials.

No matter how you see yourself, you have not seen anything yet about God's perfect purpose for your life. There is always room for a change in your relationship with God. You can still progress from good to better and from better to the very best. God's work is ever progressive.

A) THE PERMANENCE OF CHANGE

"The illiterate of the 21st century will not be those who cannot read and write, but those who cannot learn, unlearn, and relearn." — **Alvin Toffler**

The only thing stable in life is change.

When you finish changing, you are finished.

a) *The major goal of education is to change people*

Any word spoken to you that doesn't change you is useless.

When it doesn't improve you, it is worthless.

b) *Information is the building block of education*

You need new information to provoke new realisation.

You need a new revelation to attain new manifestation.

c) *The word of God is wisdom. It is profitable to direct*

Which better source do we have to shop for motivating information than the word of God?

The purpose of the scripture is to fully equip you for all good works.

All scripture is given by the inspiration of God and is profitable for doctrine, for reproof, for correction, for instruction in righteousness (2 Tim. 3:16-17.) Studying the word of God approves you for exploits in life (2 Tim.2:15.) Words work for you when you work with words!

B) THE PRINCIPLES OF CHANGE

And be not conformed to this world: but be ye transformed by the renewing of your mind, that ye may prove what is that good, and acceptable, and perfect, will of God.
Rom. 12:2

1) *God is sovereign*

God's promises are yes and Amen. Whatever God said is final. (Is 46:10)

The major source of problems on earth is human disobedience to the instructions of God.

We experience robbery and murder because a disobedient person refuses to honour God's instruction not to steal or murder.

Nations' fight wars against each other because people chose not to forgive and love each other. Most of the time, man's action is exactly the opposite of God's instruction. For us to enjoy God's promises and blessing, someone will have to change.

Since God's principles, like God, are everlasting, I guess it is the man that has to change his way to fit the ways of the Lord.

2) *Man is responsible*

Whatever you put action on is activated.

There is always something to do to enter God's promises and provision (Deut. 28:1). Man's situation on earth is mostly the direct product of his action and inaction. The reason Adam was punished in the Garden of Eden bothered on the "sovereignty of God and the responsibility of man". Because Adam deliberately refused to take responsibility to redress his sin of disobeying God by asking for forgiveness, God penalised him and Eve, his wife. Whenever you refuse to receive forgiveness, expect a consequence.

3) *Man's responsibility is a product of being a creature of free will*

No God in Heaven or satan in hell or man on earth is able to change the will of a man. That is part of the package of being created in God's image.

You are solely responsible for your life.

Unless you decide to change, nothing and nobody - no matter how great and powerful and passionate they are - can change you.

4) *Making a choice is a way of exercising your free will*

God has put you in control of your life in every situation.

Only you are responsible for your life.

Your friends and family will try to help you.

Your pastor and parents will try to influence you, but in the end, you are responsible for your race of life. It is like feeding or breathing.

You still have to do it yourself. Your faith is a personal walk with God.

If you are not completely satisfied with what you see, perhaps it is time to activate your faith and accept your responsibility to make a change.

5) *You are not a product of your circumstances, but of your choice*

So long we are alive, **chance, accident and circumstances** will sometimes bring good and bad time our way. Tough time can prove to be painfully hard. Despite these challenges of life, your destiny is finally a product of your **choice** and not that of your **circumstances**.

6) *You are in control of your situation through the choice you make*

Do not be deceived: God cannot be mocked. A man reaps what he sows (**Gal 6:7.**) Today who you are is the report sheet of the choices you made within your time limits. Your profession is what you exchanged your time for. Your house and cars are what you exchanged for the salary you received from the investment of your time.

7) *The concept of judgement comes from the need to be accountable*

You will be judged for rightly taking responsibility or not taking any responsibility. Being a creation of God demands to live under the Creator's jurisdiction of the law. (Rom. 3:19) All of God's creatures (from the stars to planetary bodies, from plants to animals and man) operate under laws. There are laws of motion, laws of chemical action and reaction, laws of mathematics, laws of love, laws of giving and faith etceteras.

While animals are instinctive, man, having the knowledge of moral laws is morally responsible for his decisions, choices and actions.

8) *Your harvest is a consequence of your seed*

There is no difficult situation that a resolute man cannot make the best out of. Jabez changed his painful existence by prayer.

He refused to organize a pity party around himself but rather chose to seek the Lord that can change all situations. Instead of Jacob to get frustrated, complaining about living in the curse, he decided to have a night of divine encounter with the Lord where he wrestled with the Lord till he was blessed (Genesis 32:22-31.) It is not the problem facing you that should determine your future; it is how you respond to it.

9) *Your time is the greatest resources (seed) you have on earth*

God has not supplied man with all his needs on earth but has rather supplied him with the earthly currency of "time" to get all he desires.

That earthly currency of time (your seed) is what you exchange for all your needs on earth (harvest.) It is the time that you invest in school to get an education. It is the time that you invest with others to build a relationship. It is the same time you invest in labour to earn a salary. Your time is simply your life and how you spend your time is how you spend your life.

10) *Life is about the choices and decisions we make daily*
80% of what happens to you in life depends on your reaction and choice. You are responsible and accountable for your decision and choice. Every man experiences problems and trials in life. That is not a problem. The problem with the problem is how we respond to it.

CHOOSE LIFE

This day I call the heavens and the earth as witnesses against you that I have set before you life and death, blessings and curses. Now choose life, so that you and your children may live. **Deut. 30: 19 (NIV)**

You are what you choose!
Because the law of change is operated by choice, it can also be called the "law of choice." Today is a product of yesterday's choice and tomorrow will be the product of today's choice. You are in the profession you are today, earning the amount you are earning because that is what you choose. Many times, life will offer you sadness, weakness and death.
It is your responsibility to choose life above that.
It is our response that can make or break us. Choose right!
Never judge your destiny by your problems, environment, limitation or status. You have great potentials in you to overcome such situations.
Even when nature deals you with the wrong cards of life, you can still win the card of choice. Quite often, one can easily be frustrated if you are handled wrongly by the following situations:

a. **Circumstances**: You might have been born in a bad environment or country that limits your ability to certain rights of life.

b. **Chemistry**: You may have been born with a challenging personality. Your height, size, colour or language may offer you hurdles to cross.

c. **Connection**: You may have different gifts and calling than others

d. **Circumstances**: You may have been born disabled, poor or in other disadvantaged condition or situation.

e. **Choice**: This is the most potent card of life that can nullify the rest.

CASE STUDY: JABEZ CHOOSE TO BE EXCELLENT!

Scripture: 1 Chronicles 4: 9-10

Jabez found himself in a sad situation; he could no more tolerate. Rather than bemoaning his situation, he chose to change it by praying. You too can do that when you are faced with the same situation. You can change the circumstances of your birth if they are not favourable. Many people change their country and nationality easily nowadays. You can also improve your personality to look healthier.

You can connect with right crowds that share the same vision of life with you in order to tap into their rich supply of experience, skill and gifts. And you can always improve your life, regardless of your disability. With technology, there is no limit. You just need to make up your mind to add value to your life through special education and training.

Where there is a will, there is always a way.

For believers, there is no limit to the level you can climb to, in the lord.

You can do all things through Jesus Christ that strengthens you.

Choose to improve your environment.

Choose to make people better and happier.

Choose to create a moment of joy in the people that cross your way.

Maximize your existence by making the world a better place.

You can make the best of your situation, only if you choose to.

If you are not comfortable with your personal circumstance in life, you have a choice. Change!

PRAYER POINTS

If any of you lack wisdom, let him ask of God, that giveth to all men liberally, and upbraideth not; and it shall be given him. 6 But let him ask in faith, nothing wavering. For he that wavereth is like a wave of the sea driven with the wind and tossed. 7 For let, not that man think that he shall receive any thing of the Lord. 8 A double minded man is unstable in all his ways. **James 1:5-8**

1. Heavenly Father, forgive me for doubting your good plans for my life. Purge my heart clean of every fear, unbelief and doubts, in Jesus, might name. Amen. (Jer.29:11)
2. I forgive every one that offends me even as I ask you, God, to forgive me all my sins in Jesus mighty name. Amen. (Mark 11:26)
3. Thank you father, for giving me the fresh grace to repent of my past and present sins. Forgive me all my trespasses in Jesus name. Amen
4. Father, grant me wisdom that will enable me to do exploits for your kingdom. (Matt.6: 33; James 1:5)
5. Father, grant me a fresh vision for my life purpose. (Hab.2:1-3)
6. Father, help me to make great choices among various opportunities coming my way daily (Deut. 30:15-19.)
7. Father, may you bless me indeed, keep me from evil, enlarge my coast and make me live an honourable life (1 Chronicles 4:9-10.)

CHAPTER 2: DISCOVERING AND DEVELOPING YOUR POTENTIALS

I praise you because I am fearfully and wonderfully made; your works are wonderful, I know that full well **Psalm 139:14 (NIV)**

You are a phenomenal expression of life.

You are fearfully and wonderfully created.

To lift up your finger alone, a scientist can document information that can fill a big library, just to explain how your body system pulls that off. That is why human best creation, the robot, is but a stiff joke of the real thing.

It takes God and you to really show who you are.

Be at home with yourself. No one can beat you in being you.

You are an ingenious creature with complex personalities.

So what is your excuse for remaining poor, frustrated or sad?

- I am not beautiful
- I am too fat, thin, short, tall, small, big, young, old
- I am married or single
- I am overworked or jobless
- I am uneducated, overeducated or educated

Now let me introduce you to yourself.

The value of a thing is determined by its rarity, not by people's opinion.

You are one in 7.2 billion possessing your unique genes and fingerprints.

You are a unique being, for there is only one of your types alive.

You are fearfully and wonderfully created.

You are the original copy of yourself.

God does not produce fake or rubbish. Everyone is created as a genius. It is a pursuit of the wrong purpose that makes an idiot out of a genius. You have an uncommon purpose awaiting uncommon rewards.

The problem is that many people have ended up as square pegs in round holes. Many are doing what they are not created to do?

Everybody has a unique assignment on earth. To flourish, every man needs to recognize his potential and be planted in an environment where it can flourish. Environment plays a great role in plant growth.

Seeds do not flourish equally in every environment. The environment where maize flourishes well is different from the environment where rice flourishes. I once read an interesting story about a penguin.

The first impression you have about a penguin is, "what a poor misconstruction with such small wings, stocky size and missing knees." You will be forced to change your mind, however, as soon as the penguin jumps into the water and begin to swim. Penguins are known to be amazing swimmers. No man or similar animals can compete with a penguin in its natural habitat.

Rather than wanting to look like others, sometimes it is better to find out your difference and the unique talent and gifts that you have that can distinguish you. Rather than limiting your life by focussing on your weaknesses, you should be maximising it by focussing more on the areas of your strength. While a penguin may not be in the same league with giraffes, elephants and lions on the land's terrain, it is not the same when it is underwater. What are your potentials? What are your strengths, skills and experiences, and what can you do with them?

Rather than staying where you are just tolerated, locate where your gift is celebrated. And when you find such an environment where your potential blossoms, celebrate the place.

It is not in every environment that you can flourish. Nothing leads to frustration, like missing the place of your blessing and flourishing.

WHAT IS POTENTIAL?

We now have this light shining in our hearts, but we ourselves are like fragile clay jars containing this great treasure. This makes it clear that our great power is from God, not from ourselves. **2 Cor.4:7 (NLT)**

Potential can be described as a hidden glory.
God hides greatness in the clay of jar called man.
This is to give all the credits of human greatness to God.
Hidden inside a baby is a woman or a man.
God hides in one family nations and generations.
Every man is packaged with a heavenly solution for earthly needs.
The potential is an unlimited resource of God in all His creation.
God hides great things in small things called potential.
For example, inside a seed are trees, fruits and uncountable generations of seeds. A tree, in essence, stores forests inside it as small as it looks.
It takes imagination to see through the seed into the forests inside it.
Inside the murderer, Moses was the Pentateuch (the 5 Old Testament books.) Inside the murderer, Saul was almost half of the New Testament.

THE PRINCIPLES OF POTENTIAL

For the kingdom of heaven is as a man travelling into a far country, who called his own servants, and delivered unto them his goods. 15 And unto one he gave five talents, to another two, and to another one; to every man according to his several ability; and straightway took his journey. **Matt. 25:14-15**

Jesus Christ taught His disciples the principles of potential through this highly enlightening parable.

1. The source of all potentials is God (Matt. 25:14; Gen. 1:1)

Like all other things in the kingdom of God, God is the source of all potentials. It was He that created heaven and earth and everything in them. God is the omnipotent - the source of all potentials and powers.

2. We do not have equal potential (Matt. 25:15)

The purpose of a product determines its potential.

Every manufacturer prepares a product for a purpose and builds in it, the potential to make that product fulfil its purpose. Every assignment also demands the unique potential that God has given into individuals.

3. In every little is many, and in every small is great (Matt. 25:16)

Genesis 1:28 implies that the ability to have dominion is in every man. All that such need to do is to be fruitful, multiply, replenish and subdue the earth (womb of the world). Every man has the responsibility to trade the potential deposited within him to enjoy the greatness in his field.

To be productive, a seed needs to develop and let out the forests inside.

4. Every creation has all required to fulfil destiny (Matt. 25:15-16)
Every product is designed with the ability to fulfil its purpose. That is called potential.

5. To develop potential is a decision of the carrier (Gen. 25:16)
That seed has the potential to produce a forest doesn't mean it will automatically do. It first needs to be planted, rooted and endure growth.

6. The undeveloped potential is a wasted resource (Gen. 25:18)
An individual needs to commit to the process of personal development to let out potential. A hidden and untapped potential is wasted.

7. We are stewards who will give an account of potentials (Gen.25:19)
God is the source of all resources, and everybody will one day give an account of stewardship to Him. Your spouse, children, business even life are not yours. They are given to you, and you will once give an account.

8. Good use of potential attracts increase (Matt. 25:20-23)
Good servants receive the compliments of the Master. When God returns, do not expect compliments for living longer than others or acquiring material wealth than others. He will judge you according to the performance of the assignment He has given you. May you hear, "well done my good servant" on that day.

But that means you will have to devote your life to doing the work of God, not yours. You could be doing the work of God for your selfish reward, and you may be doing the same job for the glory of God. It is a matter of perception and motive. God wants us to live to do His will.

9. A waste of potential attracts divine punishment (Matt. 25:24, 30) The steward who did not invest his talent dishonours God with his wrong motives and mindsets. He thought that God did not deserve the glory over his existence. The judgement of his Master was to remove his potentials and cast him away to utter destruction (Matt. 25:28-30.)

10. Fear is a major reason people hide their potentials (Matt. 25:25) God has not given us the spirit of fear but of love and a sound mind. Good reasoning comes from God. You can think your way out of any bad situation. As a man thinks, so is he (Prov. 23:7.)

Meditate on whatsoever thing that is good and of good reports (Philippians 4:8.) Meditate on the word of God to grow your faith.

You will be judged by what your gifting and calling equip you to do.

And unto one, he gave five talents, to another two, and to another one; to every man according to his several ability. **Matt 25:15**

That is good news because the greatest resources you will ever need to fulfil your life are already in you.

Fish needs not to struggle to swim, and birds need no training to fly.

Every seed carries full-blown plant within it. You only need to discover your personal endowment in life and distinguish yourself with it.

You do not need to compare yourself to anybody or compete with them. Set yourself free. Serve the Lord with the gifts you are given.

11. God expects every man to live a productive life (Matt. 25:26-27) And God blessed them, and God said unto them, be fruitful, and multiply, and replenish the earth, and subdue it: and have dominion. (Gen. 1:28a) God has given to every man the mandate to have dominion on earth. He expects us to be fruitful and multiply!

12. God of purpose loves responsible stewards (Matt. 25: 28-29)
All the stewards were rightly judged by the Master according to how they utilised their talents. The Master in this story, representing God, surely shows great appreciation and compensation to responsible stewards.
Only a bad master rewards bad stewards.
The more your ministry serves God's purpose, the more He will reward you with an increase. God honours increase with more increase.

HOW TO DISCOVER AND DEVELOP YOUR POTENTIAL[1]

"God gives talent, work transforms talent into genius."- **Anna Pavlova**

"You will be the same person in five years as you are today except for the people you meet and the books you read." — **Charlie Jones**

The followings are sure scriptural steps to release your potentials.

1. Secure genuine value for your existence

Godly principles protect you from destructive conducts and solidly plant your feet on the path of victory and success. It gives you valuable goals,

---

[1] Take a test at the back of the book (Appendix 1)

priorities and missions to live for. When you have priority in your life, it helps to focus you on achieving your purpose.

You cannot richly live until you have great values to live for. Having a great value to live for is what brings discipline and principles to your life.

One of the major weapons of the enemy against purposeful living is a distraction. Only those who maintain focus can experience a breakthrough. The more you focus on the right thing, the more the bad companies and situation will fall away from your life.

2. Recognize and celebrate your difference

God made us different one from another.

Your life was never meant to be like that of everyone else.

You are created differently, equipped differently and positioned differently to achieve a unique purpose on earth. It is your difference that distinguishes you. Your difference is for your identity.

It is also to make you relevant.

It is what creates special demands for your service.

To add value to others, you first need to recognize and celebrate your uniqueness and allow it to direct you.

The more your ministry serves God's purpose the more He will reward you with increase. God honours increase with more increase.

---

3. Take hold of your dreams and run with your vision

I will stand upon my watch, and set me upon the tower, and will watch to see what he will say unto me, and what I shall answer when I am reproved. 2 And the Lord answered me, and said, Write the vision, and make it plain upon tables, that he may run that readeth it. **Habakkuk 2:1-2**

Vision is the picture of your future!

A question of vision seeks to answer, "Where am I to go?"

Many business schools and motivational speakers have misled people about what true vision is all about. Many people have been taught wrong to think that vision is about dreaming big and earnestly desiring some type of achievement or distinction, as power, honour, fame or wealth.

That is, however, ambition, not vision.

James Collins and Jerry Porras in their 1994 book entitled "Built to Last: Successful Habits of Visionary Companies", used the term 'Big Hairy Audacious Goal' (BHAG) to encourage companies to define visionary goals that are more strategic and emotionally compelling.

Such goals are to capture great goals that such companies hope to accomplish in the future. The Bible teaches us that vision is about receiving the picture of the future from the Scripture (Bible).

It is about receiving direction for your future from the Lord.

That is why the prophet in the above scripture sought the face of the Lord for direction. You will also need to seek the face of the Lord in fasting and prayer for direction for your life. (Jer. 1:4-12)

What a shame that many have replaced godly vision for human ambition.

The importance of vision

The importance of vision is emphasised by the simple fact that you cannot pursue a future you do not see. Receiving your vision from the Lord is a good guarantee that you will not miss your destination.

Vision makes a big difference between existing and living.

The best way to break stagnation in a man's life is to show him a future.

Reaching your destination begins with a vision. God had to paint a picture of the future to Abram after his cousin left him to inspire him afresh to move on. A man robbed of vision is robbed of motivation and motion towards his future. Vision is a major source of motivation in life. Locate your assignment. Decide what is important in life. The day you find what is worth dying for or living for is the day you begin to live! Remember that every passing second brings you closer to departure.

4. Continue to develop your potentials

Work hard so you can present yourself to God and receive his approval. Be a good worker, one who does not need to be ashamed and who correctly explains the word of truth. **2 Tim 2:15 (NLT)**

Study your life manual in order to be approved. **(2 Tim 3:16-17)**
Also, study your potential. Know your abilities, resources and gifts.
Study the area of your gifting and calling.
Learners are leaders. Continuous learners make continuous leaders.
Learning is a capacity building and self-development program.
Learning adds fatness to your vision.

The Need for Capacity Development

The natural step to locating your vision is in, investing in capacity development. A question of capacity development answers the need for "filling in the gaps" between your present ability and the desired ability to reach your destination. Capacity development is about securing necessary training, education and skill required to realise your vision.

Ignorance is a robber of vision. Experience teaches that you can never go beyond your capacity development in life.

In the physical, your earning mostly is attached to your learning.

Capacity development is about stretching yourself to attain the next level. Your responsibility is to discover your potentials (gifts and callings) and develop them. Jesus Christ invested 30 years in developing Himself for his ministry of three and a half years. Paul took time out of the business of this world and prepare for his assignment. (Gal. 1:11-18)

To record success and fulfilment, you will also need to invest in your life. To earn more, you need to become more.

The need for mentorship

He that walketh with wise men shall be wise: but a companion of fools shall be destroyed. **Prov. *13:20***

Refuse self-limitation. Seek mentorship from people ahead of you!

To be outstanding in life, you need to stand out of yourself.

What a pity that many people in our generation suffer greatly from limiting themselves to their limited understanding. We now live in a self-made, self-opinionated world where many people are too proud to submit under the tutelage of other people. Be wise; expand your horizon.

5. **Develop human relationship and networks (Prov. 18:24)**

The major ingredient that you need to mix with your potential is a human relationship. We often need people to help us develop beyond ourselves. Because of the relationship Elisha had with Elijah, he was able to enter and practice a great prophetic ministry. Elisha was a business farmer turned mighty prophet. He had the double anointing upon Prophet Elijah's life simply by mastering relationship. Think about that fact for a while? The relationship that some of the disciples had with Jesus Christ changed their status from local fishermen to fishers of men.

6. **Pursue your purpose to the end with obsession (Philip. 3:13-14)**

Nothing unlocks your potential like the discovery and pursuits of your purpose. The more you pursue your calling, the more your gifts and potentials reveal. Proverbs 22:29 talks of the blessing of diligence.

A man that is diligent, skilled and obsessed in his profession will stand before kings. In essence, he will be great and well accomplished.

Are you ready for your future?

The future is not about a time, a dream or a place to come.

Rather, the future is a process to complete. It is not a destination, but a journey of several developments. It is not a dream to awake in but rather a several activities you consciously go through to make your dream come true. If you need your dream to come true, you will need to wake up and work at it. Great future only awaits those who walk towards it in faith. Plan, pursue and persist. That is the steps to your future!

PRAYER POINTS

For with God, nothing shall be impossible. **Luke 1:37**

1. Thank you, Heavenly Father, for all your promises towards me, for they are all "Yes and Amen". (2 Cor. 1:20)
2. Thank you, Father, for creating me in your image and likeness. Help me to discover, develop and deploy my potentials fully in Jesus mighty name. Amen. (Psalm 139:14)
3. God, help me to locate my purpose and discover my full potential that my life may bring you glory. (Matt. 25:16)
4. Father, make me a good steward of my gifts in my services to your kingdom and to the people of my generation. (1 Peter 4:10)
5. Father, grant me the fortitude to perfect my talents. (2 Tim. 2:15)
6. Let my diligence take me to the realm of greatness, O Lord. (Prov.22:29)
7. Thank you, my Lord, for all the good people you have given me in life to enjoy my walk of faith and faithfulness. (Prov. 27:17; 11:14)

Learners are leaders.

Continuous learners make continuous leaders.

Learning is a capacity building and self-development program. Learning adds fatness to your vision.

CHAPTER 3: DISCOVERING AND FULFILLING YOUR DESTINY

"The two most important days in your life are the day you are born, and the day you find out why." **Mark Twain**

In whom also we have obtained an inheritance, being predestinated according to the purpose of him who worketh all things after the counsel of his own will. ***Eph. 1:11***

Martin Luther junior once said, "If a man has no purpose for living, he is not fit to live for life is a burden to him because he is a burden to existence."
That is a plain fact of life supported by the Bible!
You need to locate your destiny in the purpose of God on earth before you can fulfil it. It is the timely discovery of one's destiny and the dedicated pursuit of it that gives one sure inheritance in the Lord.
There are 5 major means of discovering your destiny.[2]

1. PROPHECY

Separate me Barnabas and Saul for the work whereunto I have called them.
Acts 13:2

Many people are divinely called to their vocation in life through visions, dreams or the direct intervention of God. Sometimes, men of God will

---
[2] I treated this topic in my book, "Fulfilling Your Destiny" from page 56 -69

confirm the calling of God upon your life, but whatsoever means, you receive God's calling, you are mostly called to fulfil a specified purpose. One has to be very sure he hears the voice of God and not of his personal desire, lest he pushes himself to a place where he lacks the spiritual back-up necessary to sustain him. (1 Thess. 5: 24)

2. PRESENTS

For the gifts and calling of God are without repentance **Rom 11:29**

Another way you can find out your destiny and calling in life is through God's presents and gifts in your life.
The talents deposited in you, like any calling of God, can help you to live a profitable and valuable life. The good news is that every man is talented and able to make a living out of his talent.

And unto one he gave five talents, to another two, and to another one; to every man according to his several ability; and straightway took his journey. **Matt 25:15**

We cannot all be professors, preachers or painters, but we are all created to fulfil a purpose.
That you can talk or cram verses, do not make you a candidate for posturing if you are not called by God to do so, but we can all evangelize on the street and serve as marketplace apostles in our various working places. All you need to do is to find out where you are more gifted or talented than others and begin to serve in that area.
Your gift or talent could be a pointer to your destiny.

You need to possess distinct, or at least above average ability than others in a field, career or business before you can convert such to a profitable occupation. Follow your talent. That is a natural path to stardom.

> You need to locate your destiny in the purpose of God on earth before you can fulfill it. It is the timely discovery of one's destiny and the dedicated pursuit of it that gives one sure inheritance in the Lord.

3. PRACTICE

And I have given the Levites as a gift to Aaron and to his sons from among the children of Israel, to do the service of the children of Israel in the tabernacle of the congregation, and to make an atonement for the children of Israel: that there be no plague among the children of Israel, when the children of Israel come nigh unto the sanctuary. **Num. 8:19**

Many people inherited their professions, and they are making the best of it. The queen of England is a ruler by virtue of historical tradition and practice of Great Britain. Many people inherit their profession from their parents. The richness of the informal training they went through in their growing up, equips them with immense knowledge and experience that outside people can hardly duplicate. Even in Church institutions, many preachers simply inherited the office of their parents. It was the practice of Levites, then to be ordained as priests of the Lord.

Taking up a profession through practice, social inheritance or divine predestination could be a great way of locating destiny.

4. PASSION

Seest thou a man diligent in his business? he shall stand before kings; he shall not stand before mean men. **Prov. 22:29**

If you have passion, you can train to serve in any ministry of your choice. Passion is a great desire at achieving a goal.

It was the passion of the youthful David to rescue the people of the Lord from the hand of their boastful opponent that led him to defeat Goliath, whom many able men fled away from out of fear.

(1 Sam 17:34-37)

Passionate people are always resolute in achieving their goals.

They just couldn't get away from it.

Show me a passionate man and I will show you an achiever that would soon attain his goals. Passion is the common denominator among all inventors. Many of them were discarded as dropouts and outcasts by societies, but they nonetheless rode over their passion to great heights of dominion where champions reside.

Thomas Edison, Bill Gates, Mother Theresa, the list is without end.

5. PREFERENCE

Delight thyself also in the LORD; and he shall give thee the desires of thine heart.
5 Commit thy way unto the LORD; trust also in him; and he shall bring it to pass.

6 And he shall bring forth thy righteousness as the light, and thy judgment as the noonday. **Ps. 37:4-6**

In case you cannot choose your profession and purpose in life in all the areas enumerated above, you are lucky to have a whole spectrum of choice in front of you. Just choose where you like to distinguish yourself and commit your way to the hand of the Lord. The word of the Lord reassures that God will honour your choice and bring your heart's desire to pass. You can dream every dream you can locate in the Bible, and God will bring it to pass. What a bright future we have in the Lord!

What an unlimited prospect of progress and glamorous future we have in Christ. Many people have chosen their professions of interest and have made a great success of it.

I have travelled widely all over the world, and there is no country I have not seen people from outside that continent and race permanently settling down as citizens. That is their choice!

Regardless of where you are born, as international boundaries disappear in the corporate world, you can choose where to live and die by your preference. Most students specialize in their fields of expertise by choice. As this enlightenment comes your way from the word of the Lord, you can soberly review your life and make a choice that will enhance your value among your generation.

The eyes of your understanding being enlightened; that ye may know what is the hope of his calling, and what the riches of the glory of his inheritance in the saints

Eph. 1:18

If today, you find yourself in the wrong field you do not enjoy or you find out other areas of your life where you can live more distinguished, it is never too late to change. You are not a tree so your feet are not rooted. That you have spent a long time doing what is wrong is no reason to continue it. Free yourself from every bondage of life, be it from an external source or a self-inflicted one.

The truth of the word of God has come your way to set you free.

Relish in the hope of His calling as the eyes of your understanding becomes enlightened. You can choose to be who you want.

More so if you lack the wisdom required to make the next step, you can go on your knee right now and ask the Lord.

He has promised to give you liberally.

If any of you lack wisdom, let him ask of God, that giveth to all men liberally, and upbraideth not; and it shall be given him. **James 1:5-7**

What greatest **dream** will you fulfil if you know that you cannot fail?

Dreams are pictures of your future that God planted inside you.

It is a flash from the future. Pursue it with faith!

May every limit in your life be removed as you pursue your destiny.

You can live fulfilled too if you choose to!

You need to possess distinct or at least above average ability than others in a field, career or business before you can convert such to a profitable occupation.

Follow your talent.

That is a natural path to stardom.

THE PRINCIPLES OF DESTINY

1. God is a God of destiny

Your programmer already packaged your purpose in your microform before planting in your mother's womb. You are on earth on purpose.

2. The greatest discovery in life is personal destiny and purpose

Discovery of your destiny is your vital duty. Destiny is not decided but discovered. Although everyone and everything on earth has a purpose, this does not mean that we are aware of these purposes.
We need to seek revelation from the Lord (Maker) **Jer. 29:11-13**

3. Without locating your destiny and purpose, life becomes a painful experiment

Life has no meaning where you only exist than live. Many people become frustrated; drug addicted and often turned alcoholic, even a terrorist, etc. Where purpose is not known, abuse and misuse are inevitable. Lack of purpose is a major source of a modern day identity crisis (homosexuality), marriage crisis etc.

4. Success is about fulfilling your destiny

Success is about achieving the goal or purpose of a thing.
Birds must fly, fish must swim, and man must grow up to a mature adult.
We rejoice when our body parts fulfil their purpose.
They become liabilities when they no more perform their functions.
We cut them off only when they malfunction.

5. **Being successful in your destiny is a step to fulfilling God's purpose for your life**

Being good in your personal destiny helps you to be valuable unto a godly purpose. You can't be a bad worker and hope to be a good minister of God (Rom. 12:11). Do not be slothful in business and fervent in spirit. Let your performance testify well for your faith.

6. **Life fulfilment comes from achieving your life purpose**

Everything with destiny has a purpose. It is the destiny of a Coca-Cola bottle to carry coke drink, and the purpose is for people to drink. It's a disaster if the bottle carries drink for 100 years and nobody drinks it. Destiny and purpose are two sides of the same coin.

The purpose of life is to use your destiny to fulfil God's purpose.

May you not just fulfill your destiny in life, but may you use it to fulfil God's purpose. May you not just be a good teacher, but be a godly teacher. May you not just be a good parent, but the godly parent.

> **Everything with destiny has a purpose. It is the destiny of Coca-Cola bottle to carry Coke drink and the purpose is for people to drink. It's a disaster if the bottle carries drink for 100 years and nobody drinks it. Destiny and purpose are two sides of the same coin. The purpose of life is to use your destiny to fulfil God's purpose.**

PRAYER POINTS

Ask, and it shall be given you; seek, and ye shall find; knock, and it shall be opened unto you: 8 For every one that asketh receiveth; and he that seeketh findeth; and to him that knocketh it shall be opened. **Matt 7:7-8**

1. Father, Lord, by your mighty power and by the power in the Blood of Jesus and the Fire of Holy Ghost, scatter and destroy any evil spirit hindering my progress in life. (Isaiah 54:15)

2. Let every power, making a decree to affect my standing in the Lord, be terminated, in the name of Jesus. (Isaiah 54:17)

3. By the power of the Holy Spirit, cause me to discover and live fully my destiny O Lord. (Matt. 25:15)

4. Father, Lord, let my feet be anointed and washed by your blood to lead me to my wealthy realms, in the name of Jesus. (Eph. 1:3)

5. I receive today, the passion and persistence to fulfil my dreams and visions in Jesus mighty name. Amen. (Hab. 2:1-3)

6. The power to succeed in life; come upon me now, in Jesus' name.

7. Power to overcome, fall upon me now, in the name of Jesus.

What greatest dream will you fulfil if you know that you cannot fail? Dreams are pictures of your future that God planted inside you.
It is a flash from the future. Pursue it with faith!

CHAPTER 4: DISCOVERING AND FULFILLING YOUR PURPOSE

And we know that all things work together for good to them that love God, to them who are the called according to his purpose. **Rom. 8:28 (KJV)**

While your potentials are helpful hints to locate your destiny, your destiny is a great platform to discover your purpose. That means while locating your potentials and destiny, the same path you take can lead to discovering and fulfilling your purpose in life. That is how it worked out from my personal experience.

I started teaching primary school students needing extra coaching hours after leaving secondary school. In the Church, I was allocated the duty to lead Sunday Schools. In the later stage of my post-graduate career in the bank, I was allocated to the Education and Training department, where I engaged in training senior bank executives.

Since I joined the full-time ministry, my roles and duties as a Pastor and Bible school lecturer have focused mostly on teaching.

You see, all things work together for good to prepare you for your purpose. Even your mistakes, trials and challenges will work together for good so long you keep your sight glued to fulfilling your purpose.

A) LOCATING YOUR PURPOSE

In addition to taking the five steps of locating your destiny, there are other additional steps you can take to locate your life purpose.

1) Take note of the areas of your talents and spiritual gifts

Make social and spiritual gift tests or inventories[3].

What does it reveal to you about yourself?

2) Identify the area of pain or spiritual attacks

While it is true that your area of strength can reveal your life purpose, it is equally true that your area of greatest threat and attack could also reveal your purpose as seen in the lives of Moses and Gideon (Exodus 6:30; Judges 6:12-16.) Moses was a stammerer though he was meant to be a statesman. Gideon was a weakling though he was meant to be a warrior and a deliverer of his people. Many healing and miracle ministers began their life as a chronic sick case.

3) Take note of prophetic vision or prayers made for you

God can open you up to your next phase in life through prophetic utterance as He did to Saul. It is good also to be open to confirmation of your area of calling for people very close to you (be it your spouse, brethren or your pastor.)

4) Focus on general purpose as means to your particular purpose

Every Christian has a general purpose to do. By obediently doing this, you will notice an area of personal calling that brings you joy than other services. The general area of service for all Christians include:

---

[3] Spiritual test to discover your area of calling is attached at the end of the book.

a) We are called to seek first the kingdom of God and His righteousness (Matt. 6:33). As you do this, you will find your own place in the kingdom.
b) We are all sent out to reach for lost souls (Acts 1:8; Matt. 28:19). As we devote our lives to this, God will reveal other areas of gifting and service to us individually.
c) We are all meant to support the upkeep of the Church by giving faithfully our tithes and offerings and involving in another kingdom investment (Luke 16:11.) As we show our love to God, through obedience, he will show us clearly our personal callings and purpose.
d) We are all called to love God and our neighbours. (Matt. 22:36-40) As we do this, we will see clearly our personal role in the body of Christ. Most great men of God were running after the general-purpose when God gave them personal callings. (Matt. 4:19)

5) Keep serving the Lord

Start serving with what you have wherever you are. 1 Pet. 4:10
Be obedient to God's general instruction (Is. 1:19) for he that is faithful in little is already considered to be faithful in much.
Continue to serve God. Let Him continue to lead you.

6) Be open to new pursuits

See, I am doing a new thing! Now it springs up; do you not perceive it? I am making a way in the wilderness and streams in the wasteland **Is. 43:19**
Do not be satisfied with your past and present accomplishment.

Brothers and sisters, I do not consider myself yet to have taken hold of it. But one thing I do: Forgetting what is behind and straining toward what is ahead, 14 I press on toward the goal to win the prize for which God has called me heavenward in Christ Jesus. **Philip. 3:13-14**

7) Ask purpose revealing questions

There are seven powerful questions of life that anyone who wants to do exploits on earth and be fulfilled thereafter should answer.

B) ASKING PURPOSE DISCOVERY QUESTIONS

A) Where am I from?

This is a question of source. Who is your creator?

If you believe in Evolution theory that you are a product of the Big Bang (chaotic explosion), you will suffer identity crisis all the days of your life. If you believe that you evolve from monkeys, then your case is hopeless. Just live for now for your life is insignificant and you give an account to nobody afterwards. That is the goal of evolution theorists.

They want you to live your life fearing nothing. There is no life after death, and there is no judgement because there is no God.

What a devious deception to lure people to hell.

If you do not know where you are coming from, you can't figure out who you are and where you are going.

B) Who am I?

This is a question of identity. It is a question that reveals the authority backing you up. When I introduce myself as Solomon Osoko, I am revealing the identity of my father. If you are not satisfied, you can ask for my identity card or passport to see the government backing me up. Do you notice that immigration officers treat differently, different nationalities? If the government of your country is not internationally respected, you will be easily molested. But if your country or government is honourable, you will be equally respected.

Self-identity determines your self-worth. Many are living under the inferiority complex. Thank God that when a man is in Jesus Christ, he is a new creature (2 Cor. 5:17.) You are not just a citizen of an earthly nation; you are a citizen of heaven, a member of God's family.

Your new identity should imbue you with great confidence.

C) Why am I here?

This is a question of "purpose, importance and impact" that answers, "Why am I unique? You existed on purpose and will one day give an account to your creator (Jer. 1:5)

D) Am I doing the right thing?

This is a question of destiny. It is also the question of effectiveness.
Are you doing the right thing you are created to do?
Are you doing the right work? If not, you will always feel frustrated.
Your work is a process of releasing your potential (future).

Works are meant to release the trees inside your seed.

Labour is the laboratory to develop your negative to the colourful picture. The negative is like your potential while your future is a colourful future. To move from potential to perfection requires processing. Labour is another name for processing your potential.

Are you working or jobbing?

If your labour is not directed at perfecting your potential, you are not working but jobbing. While God gives man work (even before the downfall of sin) to reveal his potential and creativity, Pharaoh created jobs to molest people and keep them struggling for daily food.

While it might not be wrong to be engaged in a job as the situation may warrant, it is very wrong not to invest in your work. You can do both together till you secure enough financial freedom to focus on your work.

While work is unique to your gift and calling, a job is a routine that does not develop your potential. Products of such routine are ordered in large quantities and require no unique skill or expertise. It is the era of job that makes it possible to sack people in large numbers. It is that same era that we began to use machine terms for people like downsizing,

The arrival of super computers would soon worsen the situation.

Only those who stick to their areas of unique gifting may find it easier to survive. The truth is that a computer may be able to do work of a hundred unskilled labourers, but a hundred computers can still not do the work of one gifted and talented person. How many computers do you think can beat late Michael Jackson in the field of his type of entertainment?

The difference is clear since there is no basis for comparison.
Our challenge is to locate ourselves in the areas of our gifting.
Remember, we are all wonderfully and fearfully created.

E) Am I doing the most I can do now?

This is a question of potential (ability) that answers, "Do I possess sufficient ability to do what I do?"

It is also the question of efficiency at work and in a career.

"Am I giving my best to what I am doing?"

F) Am I living, right?

This is a question of impact. Your gift and diligence may get you into a place, but only your attitudes can determine your altitude. (Gen. 41:38.)

Trust is one of the greatest assets you have in life.

When it is tight, can you act, right?

Can people trust you and relate with you on the long term?

G) Where am I going?

This is a question of legacy: Are you living the way you want to be remembered by man and judged by God?

How would I be remembered or judged by history?

LIVING PURPOSEFULLY

Many are the plans in a person's heart, but it is the Lord's purpose that prevails. **Prov. 19:21**

Of all human schemes, only those that correspond with the purpose of God will prevail. Purpose is the original intent for the creation of a thing in the mind of the creator. Be wise, swim with the tide.

Understand the priority of God's purpose. We can make all the plans we want in life, but if we don't make our plan's according to the purpose for which God created us, then our plan's will be in vain. Man proposes God, disposes. The man's plan is inferior to God's purpose.

The priority of purpose is also a sure ground for every child of God to celebrate. Whatever is the plan of the devil or any of his human agents, God is committed to seeing His purpose for your life fulfilled.

Stop giving the enemy a cheap opportunity to molest your life and derail God's program for your life. Sin is a trap of hell. Sin is a killer of potential, destroyer of destiny and robber of purpose.

Stay with the Lord. If God is for you, nobody can be against you.

God is determined to fulfil His purpose.

THE PRINCIPLES OF PURPOSE

1. God is a God of purpose (Jer. 1:5)

God created on purpose. He does nothing without purpose. Not one person on earth is without God's purpose.

2. **We are all living here on assignment (Jer. 1:5)**
You are not here by accident; you are here on assignment.

3. **The greatest discovery in life is your purpose (Jer.1:5)**
Your purpose can only be discovered, not decided.
No product determines own purpose.

4. **The greatest source of frustration is living without purpose**
The greatest tragedy in life is not death; it's life without purpose.
Purpose gives meaning to existence.

5. **Abortion of purpose is a frustration of perfection** (Jer. 29:11)
Abortion is not the termination of a baby, but the termination of a destiny. The kid you terminate is someone's spouse, family patriarch, nations etc. Imagine Mary aborting Jesus Christ!

6. **God's purpose is pre-eminent over man's purpose** (Prov. 19: 21)
God's general purpose for mankind is bigger than individual plans and purpose. Even though He makes known the end from the beginning, nothing can change His plan (Is. 46: 10-11.) Even though heaven and earth shall pass away, none of what God said shall go unaccomplished (Matt. 5: 18-49.) His purpose is more solid than rock and surer than human existence. Personal accomplishment fades out to utter rubbish beside the purpose of God.

7. Living in God's purpose is the key to fulfilment (Rom.8:28)

God honours your choice to be useful and successful in your career, family, and other choices you make in life so long you see, such as a means to an end. Fulfilling divine purpose for your life is about using your personal destiny to fulfil the will of God on earth.

8. If you want to know a purpose for a thing, ask its Maker (Jer. 29:11-13)

Only the maker of a thing knows its purpose, never ask a thing!
Purpose is only found in the mind of the maker (manual).

9. The best repairer of a thing is also its Manufacturer.

Only the manufacturer can repair a thing perfectly. If you go to an unauthorized dealer, you are destroying the products. Your duty is to treat the product according to the instruction of the manufacturer.
The warranty is only useful when you obey the instruction.

10. Divine direction is key to purposeful living (Ps. 127:1)

Divine direction is a spiritual guide to your destination
Learn to submit your will to do God's will, and nothing can halt your progress in life (Rom.8:31). Jesus was only able to accomplish His life purpose when He completely submitted His will to fulfil God's will (Luke 22:42; John 10:18; 1 John 3:16).

PRAYER POINTS

There are many devices in a man's heart; nevertheless the counsel of the LORD, that shall stand. **Prov. 19:21**

1. Father, Lord, scatter and destroy the power of devouring spirit and limitation, in my life in the name of Jesus Christ. Amen. (Psalm 18:37)
2. Grant me a new revelation of my status as a new creation in Jesus Christ and as a bona fide son of God. (2 Cor. 5:17)
3. God Almighty, help me to submit my will to pursue your will in Jesus mighty name. (Matt. 6:10)
4. Spirit of the Living God, arise and take me to my place of blessing now, in Jesus mighty name. (Psalm 143:12)
5. O Lord, make me live for the progress of your kingdom, for the rest of my lifetime. (Matt.6:33)
6. I receive uncommon faith to pursue my purpose to the end. (Hab.2:3-4)
7. I receive uncommon favour to fulfil my purpose in Jesus mighty name. Now, Father, let your purpose for my life be fulfilled. (Prov. 19:21)

Trust is one of the greatest assets you have in life.

When it is tight, can you act right?

Can people trust you and relate with you on a long term?

CHAPTER 5: LIVING FULFILLED

And we know that all things work together for good to them that love God, to them who are the called according to his purpose. **Rom. 8:28**

God's purpose is the platform where everything God created is fulfilled. If you locate your purpose in the unfailing purpose of God that cannot fail, then you shall no more fail in life. Great people of the Bible (like Prophet Moses, Apostle Peter and Paul, even, Our Lord Jesus Christ) are not only principled, they also locate their purpose in God's agenda for mankind and fulfil it.

There must be something you can also do in your family, church, organisation or city (politics) for the glory of God.

You are protected, blessed as long as you live on purpose.

Become a person of purpose who lives to do the will of God.

THE TWO JOHNS

There are many devices in a man's heart; nevertheless the counsel of the LORD, that shall stand. **Prov. 19:21**

Did all the acclaimed superstars, celebrities and human heroes who lived famous fulfil their destinies?

Getting the right answer to that question depends on your perspective.

Are you viewing the situation from a social or spiritual perspective?

Are you looking from human or God's point of view?

That question explains why we sometimes have confusion between the definition of destiny and purpose. As close as they are, by now, you know they are not the same thing. Let us take a cursive look at true life stories of two great men to make a clear illustration of this point.

John Lennon (1940-1980)

John Lennon was the famous British leader of Beatles' who led such a spectacular celebrity life. In 1972, John Lennon, who once boasted that his musical group, the Beatles, was more popular than Jesus wrote a desperate letter to Evangelist Oral Roberts confessing his dependence on drugs and his fear of facing up to "the problems of life." He wanted to know if Jesus could love and grant him the way "out of hell." After a few contacts with Oral Roberts, John Lennon announced in the spring of 1977 that he'd become a born-again Christian.

He was later to turn his back to Jesus, calling himself a born-again pagan. At the peak of his career, while enjoying great wealth and popularity, he sank into a deep depression. According to the book "The Gospel according to the Beatles "written by Steve Turner, John Lennon suddenly felt concerned that "his creativity had deserted him and that he had no real purpose in life." From then on, he started to worry about "his health and his eyesight, about making the right investments with his money, about his personal safety. The only way out, as far as he could see, was to pay for the services of people who claimed to see into the future. But then, which ones could he trust? If the advice of the tarot card reader contradicted that of the astrologer, which should he follow? Instead of the freedom he wanted when he broke away from the Beatles, he was now completely enslaved."

He was later shot to death by one of his fans in 1980.

John Lennon died at the age of forty, highly successful but unfulfilled.

John Rockefeller Snr. (1839-1937)

John Rockefeller was a renowned American industrialist and oil magnate.

Though his mum raised him in the strictest Baptist faith, he was noted to be greedy of money since his childhood.

He used to buy candies wholesale to resell them to his siblings at a profit. As an adult, he was able to save from his meagre income and later go into the oil business. John D.Rockefeller, as head of a booming Standard Oil Company, was accused of crushing out the competition, getting rich on rebates from railroads, coercing rivals to join his oil trust under threat of being forced out of business and building up enormous fortunes on the ruins of other men. His life was busy and stressful that no doctor gave him a chance to live long.

In 1896 at the age of 57, he gave up his career to regain his health.

He also changed his focus from making money to giving out money to needy institutions and people.

His health began to improve as he located a new purpose for himself in life. John Rockefeller, who had been the greatest "getter" of money in the country during the years he was exploiting oil resources, became, after his retirement from business, the world's greatest "giver".

In his new role as a philanthropist, where he was to live an additional forty years, he gave away over 530 million dollars to various charitable and educational organisations.

John Rockefeller passed away on his bed at the age of 97, highly successful and fulfilled.

Comparing the lives of the two Johns

1. **Both men enjoyed success in their fields, but what about their divine purposes?**
a) None of these men served as an evangelist or pastor. Only a few are called to that office. However, we all have the calling to testify about the good news of salvation to our world.
b) Rockefeller fulfilled this purpose in his role as a philanthropist and till today is still celebrated as a great citizen of earth.

   John Lennon could have served God's purpose also by using his God-given talents to praise the Lord and testify to other people.

   He, however, chose to use his talents for his career only and publicly denied the existence of God.

   You will find various similar examples everywhere around you today.

2. **To enjoy a truly fulfilling life, you need to use personal purpose (your destiny) to achieve God's purpose (divine destiny) by attending to your calling with your gifts.**
a) While God has given you several gifts to enjoy your personal purpose, He has also called you to use your success to pursue His purpose. That explains why a man considered very successful in his field could feel like a titanic failure if his private success is not used to accomplish the shared goals of other people.
b) Joy will evade such a man, regardless of any happiness he might enjoy from things happening around him. Though your occupation might keep you happy and busy, only the kingdom work keeps you joyful and fulfilled.

3. **True destiny is the one located in the purpose of God**
a) What shall it profit a man who gained the whole world and loses his soul? It doesn't matter what your fans and friends say. God's verdict is the final.

b) Until your purpose is located in God's purpose, no matter the success you witness in your private life and career, it is in vain. Every other achievement should be used as a means to fulfil God's purpose in your life. That is what purposeful living is all about.

4. **Your true purpose in life is in divine destiny**
a) God's purpose for your life is bigger than your personal destiny and purpose. You are created to solve other people's problem.
b) Your financial rewards, social eminence and spiritual accomplishment, are all attached to your finding out God's purpose for your life and fulfilling it.
c) Purpose fulfilment negates all the mistakes and problems of life and adds up to your success. All things work out together for good on the platform of purpose (Rom. 8:28.)

> **Until your purpose is located in God's purpose, no matter the success you witness in your private life and career, it is in vain. Every other achievement should be used as a means to fulfil God's purpose in your life.**

THE RELATIONSHIP BETWEEN DESTINY AND PURPOSE

For God's gifts and his call can never be withdrawn. **Rom. 11:29 (NLT)**

There is a relationship between destiny and purpose, and we can demonstrate an example from the Life of Jesus Christ.

a) **Destiny**: Jesus Christ was born to die for the sins of mankind (The wages of sin is death. Rom. 6:23a)

b) **Purpose**: The purpose of the death of Jesus Christ on the cross of Calvary was to fulfil **God's purpose** for human redemption.

1. Destiny is a step to fulfil your purpose

a) The same way gifts prepare you for your destiny does your destiny prepares you to fulfil your purpose. (Luke 12:16-21; 1 Tim. 6:17)

b) The purpose of destiny is to fulfil the purpose of God. While destiny is about fulfilling your personal purpose, life purpose is about fulfilling God's purpose.

2. Destiny has to do with your profession and personal survival while purpose has to do with your selfless contribution to human agenda

a) **Destiny is for your livelihood** (source of living)

- *Luke 19:13 And he called his ten servants, and delivered them ten pounds, and said unto them, Occupy till I come.*

- *Eccl. 5:19* *Every man also to whom God hath given riches and wealth, and hath given him power to eat thereof, and to take his portion, and to rejoice in his labour; this is the gift of God.*

b) **Purpose is your service to God and humanity** (what you live for)

- *2 Tim. 1:9* *Who hath saved us, and called us with an holy calling, not according to our works, but according to his own purpose and grace, which was given us in Christ Jesus before the world began.*

- *Phil. 3:13-14* *Brethren, I count not myself to have apprehended: but this one thing I do, forgetting those things which are behind, and reaching forth unto those things which are before, I press toward the mark for the prize of the high calling of God in Christ Jesus.*

3. **Destiny grants you personal income and human appreciation while purpose grants you fulfilment and eternal reward from God (1 Thess. 5:24)**

a) Destiny deals with your employment while purpose deals with your deployment.

b) Deployment is about distributing persons or forces systematically or strategically. It is about the relocation of forces and material to a desired operational area. It is to get a thing ready to be used.

4. **Destiny is a means to fulfil your God-given purpose**

a) Everything with destiny has a purpose.

Your destiny is a step to fulfil your purpose. You can't be a bad worker and hope to be good (minister of God).

b) Being good in your personal destiny helps you to be valuable for godly purposes. For you to serve your godly purpose, you first need to be good in your destined purpose. Your excellence in the fulfilment of your destiny is what brings glory to God.

Our purpose is to be advertised not only as good professionals but as godly professionals.

5. Success is about reaching your goals while fulfilment is achieving your Maker's goals

a) Success is about fulfilling destiny, while fulfilment comes from achieving the purpose.

b) You cannot substitute fulfillment with usefulness, success or being wealthy.

I could use my suit to sweep floors, and it will still be useful and perhaps successful, but it will not be fulfilling its maker's purpose. That is why many so called successful people are not fulfilled.

You're to use your accomplishment in your field to fulfil God's purpose. Understanding the roles of gifts and calling in your life will help you to do exploits.

PRAYER POINTS

And this is the confidence that we have in him, that, if we ask any thing according to his will, he heareth us: 15 And if we know that he hear us, whatsoever we ask, we know that we have the petitions that we desired of him. **1 John 5:14-15**

1. Father, the Lord, cause me to live for your purpose in Jesus mighty name. Amen. (Rom 8:28)

2. Cause me to value my soul that any other thing in this world. May your grace upon my life never be in vain. (Mark 8:36)

3. I declare that the enemy is permanently denied access to my life and destiny. I maintain by faith, my position in Jesus Christ in the heavenly places, far above all power and principalities. (Eph. 1:21)

4. I walk in dominion, power, and God's purpose. (Rom. 8:31)

5. I declare that my prophetic destinies and purposes will be fulfilled now without delay or interference. (Psalm 138:8)

6. I declare that open doors and uncommon favour in high places shall manifest continually in my life. (Psalm 5:12)

7. In the name of Jesus Christ, may divine blessings of the LORD locate and overtake me in every circumstance, business transaction, and all my relationships. Amen. (Psalm 23:1-6)

CHAPTER 6: LIVING LARGE AS PRIESTS AND KINGS

And hath made us kings and priests unto God and his Father; to him be glory and dominion for ever and ever. Amen. **Rev. 1:6**

And hast made us unto our God kings and priests: and we shall reign on the earth. *Rev. 5:10*

Every redeemed man is created as a prophet, priest and king after the order of Jesus Christ.

As a Prophet, Jesus offered His life and rose up to be High Priest under the New Covenant. He was crowned as king in crucifixion as a shadow of His reign at the end of the Age (Rev. 5:8-14.)

a) **Prophet:**

Jesus acted as the Mediator between God and man, speaking to the latter in the Name of the Former (Deuteronomy 18:15-22).

He was the God's mouthpiece and spoke only what he has heard by inspiration from God (Jeremiah 1:9; Isaiah 6:5-10; John 8:26), or what God has shown him by a vision or a dream (Num. 12:6; John 5:19-20.)

- The whole believers have been called into the prophetic office now.
- The only reason we are left in the world after our salvation is to witness to the world.

I. The fivefold ministers are prophets to the Church

II. The congregation are market place apostles witnessing to the world.

b) **King:**

A king is a mediator of the judicial and executive Power of God among His people. A king is also a judge (2 Chr. 19:6; Ps 2:10-11; John 5:27).
We are heaven's ambassadors on earth **(2 Cor. 5:17-20)**
The implication of this reality is that we are God's representatives on earth.

a) **We are God's ambassadors!**

2 Cor. 5:20 Now then we are ambassadors for Christ, as though God did beseech you by us: we pray you in Christ's stead, be ye reconciled to God.

We are His voice, hands, feet, and whatever we have or do should be to enforce His rules and desires on earth (not ours).

We are not owners but stewards of whatever we have and whatever we do, we should do it knowing we will once give account to Him.

b) **We should stop thinking locally and start thinking globally**

Stop being self-centered and permit your thinking to be, "other people centred." God is global. He thinks about the whole world.

Jesus Christ did not die for Christians alone.

He died for the whole world.

Until the final day of judgement, we need to see the whole world as the sheepfold of God. There is no goat yet, until the final judgement day.

We are all potential candidates for heaven.

We are all entitled to the unconditional love of Jesus Christ.

FINDING YOUR PLACE IN YOUR CHURCH

For as we have many members in one body, but all the members do not have the same function, so we, being many, are one body in Christ, and individually members of one another.' **Romans 12:4-5 (NIV)**

"No man has ever risen to the real stature of spiritual manhood until he has found that it is finer to serve somebody else than it is to serve himself." **Woodrow Wilson (1856 - 1924)**

The same way it is vital for every believer to be a member of a local body of Christ is it important to find a role to play as a committed member of that body.

1) WHY ENEMY DO NOT WANT YOU PLANTED IN YOUR CHURCH

Disorderly people never belonged to any church, never led any ministry, never stayed committed to anything and never believed in God enough to pay their tithes. In most cases, they complain against every man of God and every form of authority they ever came across. Their opinions change according to their emotions and conditions. They change stands on issues as soon as they collect new information being not well rooted in biblical doctrines and yet always anxious to speak. I asked one of them one day if he honours his leaders in family and office. He said yes. I asked him if that disturbed him from honouring God. He said no. When I asked him to explain to me how honouring church leadership should translate to dishonouring God who appointed them there, he had no answer. Brethren, do not permit yourself to be confused by people who are confused themselves.

Blessed is the man that walketh not in the counsel of the ungodly, nor standeth in the way of sinners, nor sitteth in the seat of the scornful. But his delight is in the law of the LORD; and in his law doth he meditate day and night. And he shall be like a tree planted by the rivers of water, that bringeth forth his fruit in his season; his leaf also shall not wither; and whatsoever he doeth shall prosper. **Psalm 1:1-3**

The righteous shall flourish like the palm tree: he shall grow like a cedar in Lebanon. Those that be planted in the house of the LORD shall flourish in the courts of our God. They shall still bring forth fruit in old age; they shall be fat and flourishing. **Psalm 92:12-14**

There are certain entitlements that naturally belong to you as a member of the body of Christ.

The only way the enemy can deny you of them is by detaching you from the main body of Christ. Be not fooled by any of his tricks and devices.

a) The church is the official registration centre where people from every walk and area of life are registered into God's book of life. (1 Cor. 1: 21; rev 3: 5, Rev 13. 8, Rev 20:12).

b) The church provides you spiritual renewal that helps you to assume the role of a Son of God. When you gave your life to Jesus, your spiritual status changed, but your physical and emotional being remained the same. You have the responsibility of renewing your mind to become the true person God created you to be (Eph. 4:23-27; 2 Cor. 10:4-6).

c) The church is the restaurant for your spiritual nourishment. You are entitled to spiritual nourishment (bread of life) that makes you strong and virile in the Lord. (James 1: 8).
d) The church is the building centre for your faith. (Heb. 6:12).
e) The church is your security wall against the attacks of the enemy. (Prov. 11: 14; Rom 8: 31).
- God has promised to build His Church (that is the congregation). So long you belong; no gate of hell can prevail upon your life.
f) The church is your training camp where your talents are detected; developed and utilised.
- The church's duty is to find out your calling, equip you and support you to fulfil it so every member can be blessed together (1 Cor. 12:24-28).
g) The church is your healing centre. (Matt. 10:8; James 5: 13-16.9).
h) The church offers you dependable lifetime companions that will partake in your eternal life (Prov. 18: 24; Rom. 12: 15).
i) The church prepares you to flourish in every area of life (Exodus 23: 24-25; Ps. 92:13).
j) The church offers you regular entrance into the presence of the Lord where there is the fullness of joy (Ps. 16: 11).

2) DEVELOPING YOUR STAYING POWER

Declaring the end from the beginning, and from ancient times the things that are not yet done, saying, My counsel shall stand, and I will do all my pleasure. **Isa. 46:10**
God's counsel will always stand!
Anything He says will happen regardless of how long it takes.

That is because He is the Alpha and Omega, the beginning and the end. Because He knows all things and creates all things, you can be rest assured that anything He promises you or says in His word will come to pass. It is left for you to develop the staying power to wait until you receive from Him.

Farmers are great people who plant their seeds and go on to prepare for the harvest even before the seeds show proof of growing up. They so much trust God's handling of natural laws that they never bothered to doubt if the sun or rain will come or not. It is a shame that many Christians have not learnt to trust God for their lives the way farmers trust Him for their harvest. Only if some of us will trust God like we trust our bosses at work, things will work better for us. Do you know of people who take credit to buy houses, cars and other materials only because they are employed? They feel secure because a man promises to pay their salary, yet this man may die, or his business may go bankrupt the next day. God is eternal, and His promises are forever valid. Yet, many will not completely entrust their hopes, aspirations and entire life in His hands. Mature faith will trust and remain in the Lord regardless of any situation. After 25 years of waiting, Abraham received the promise of God. That was because He persevered! Never give up. God is faithful; He cannot and will not fail. He always arrives on the scene on time!

3) CHURCH'S SERVICE FOR YOUR GROWTH

Following are some of the reasons you need to fellowship and worship with other believers in a Church that preaches believes and practices undiluted words of God.

A. Doctrinal

All scripture is given by inspiration of God, and is profitable for doctrine, for reproof, for correction, for instruction in righteousness: That the man of God may be perfect, throughly furnished unto all good works. **2 Tim 3:16-17**

Your church equips you with salient doctrine necessary to help you fulfil God's vision for that ministry in general and for your life in particular. Your being a Son of God is as real as your being alive. It doesn't depend on your thoughts or feelings but on the unbreakable word of God.

As you daily nourish, your spirit man with the word of God, all areas of your life will be aligned with the expectation of God concerning you.

B. Fellowship

Not forsaking the assembling of ourselves together, as the manner of some is; but exhorting one another: and so much the more, as ye see the day approaching.
Heb. 10:25

We need to fellowship together for many reasons.

a) You are a member of God's spiritual family with other Christians

For it became him, for whom are all things, and by whom are all things, in bringing many sons unto glory, to make the captain of their salvation perfect through sufferings.
Heb. 2:10

i) We are one family in Christ. (Rom. 12: 5; Eph. 2: 19b)

ii) You are called not only to believe, but also to belong together in the family. As a newly born kid needs nurturing from a particular family, so does every Christian has a need to obtain spiritual nurturing from a local fellowship. (1 Cor. 12:12; Eph. 2:21-22; 3:6; 4:1; Col 2:19; 1 Thess. 4:17, Rom 12:5)

b) You are a part of God's eternal family

i) Our relationship outlives this life. We are meant to be together forever. (Eph. 1:5 - 14)

ii) Your love for the brethren is proof of your love for God. (Matt 25:40; 1 John 4:12; John 13:35).

c) Jesus relates to His Church

i) Every genuine Christian is a part of the body of Christ. (2 Cor.11:2; Eph.5: 27, Rev.19:7)

ii) Jesus gave His life for His church. (Eph. 5:25)

iii) Jesus promises to build His Church and return for it. (Matt 16:18)

d) Special blessings of being a member of a Church

i) You prove your conviction in being a practising member of a local Church. (John 4:12; John 13:35)

ii) Our love for another proves our discipleship. (Gal 3: 28, John 17: 21)

iii) We are to complement each other's effort. (1 John 3:1; Eph. 4:1b)

iv) We can use our gifts to bless the whole body of Christ. (1 Cor. 12:7)

v) God works through us as a body. (Eph. 2:10)

vi) Assured victory in the Lord is for the Church. (Heb.12: 22-24)

vii) You can tap into the healing anointing made available to the Church. (James 5: 13-16)

C. Prayer (for divine provision, protection, intervention, security, supports, etceteras)

Praying always with all prayer and supplication in the Spirit, and watching thereunto with all perseverance and supplication for all saints. **Eph. 6:18**

And he said unto them; This kind can come forth by nothing, but by prayer and fasting. **Mark 9:29**

Prayer is the most powerful thing you can do with your mouth. Seek to build yourself up in the Lord by cultivating a daily habit of seeking His face. This way, you do not only live in His presence but also learn to recognise His voice and powerful presence in your life.

Prayer can be made more effective when offered with a forgiving heart, agreement with others and with full faith on God's unfailing mercy.

As you invite the Holy Spirit to your life and pray in the spirit, you can witness even a far rewarding and powerful prayer life.

Confess your faults one to another, and pray one for another, that ye may be healed. The effectual fervent prayer of a righteous man availeth much. **James 5:16**

Prayer made a great difference in the Pentecostal days and will still make much difference in our world today. Learn to have your quiet hours in the presence of the Lord, first thing in the morning and last thing in the day. Only then can you be sure to work in the guidance and blessing of your heavenly father who is swift to listen to His children.

D. Evangelism

There is joy in the presence of the angels of God over one sinner that repenteth. **Luke 15:10**

Jesus' last commission was for all men to become soul winners.

One major way you can demonstrate your belief in God is to witness to others through church outreach and personal conducts that attract other people to Christ. Yes, every Christian is God's ambassador on earth.

We all have the corporate calling to spread the good news of salvation around the world.

We are therefore Christ's ambassadors, as though God were making his appeal through us. **2 Cor. 5:20**

Hell is real, and so is heaven.

As Christ ambassadors on earth, it is our calling as a Church to return the lost sheep back to their Shepherd. Together we can depopulate hell and cause endless joy to erupt in heaven as multitudes of sinners' return back home to their Heavenly Father.

4) LOCATING YOUR SERVICE TO YOUR CHURCH

Therefore go and make disciples of all nations, baptizing them in the name of the Father and of the Son and of the Holy Spirit. **Matt.28:19 (NIV)**

Every believer is expected to attend Church regularly and financially support the church. More than that, every mature believer is expected to use his/her gifts and talents to serve in any of their church ministries.

Otherwise, the church will never be any stronger than its core of lay ministers who carry out the various ministries of the church.

1) Every believer is a minister. (Mark 10:45)
a) Every member of the Church has been called and sent by the Lord Jesus Christ into lay ministry. (John 14:12-14; John 20:21)
b) Every born again believer is called (I Pet. 2:9-10), gifted (I Pet. 4:10), authorized (Matt. 28:18-20), commanded to minister to the world. We are the apostles of the marketplace and have our pulpits in our various areas of work, career, play etc.

2) Every ministry is important (I Cor. 12:18-22)
- No calling is low. Every discovered purpose is a high calling.

3) Every member of the body of Christ is dependent on each other (1 Cor. 12:15-21).

4) Your ministry is the expression of your SHAPE (Rom. 12:1-8)
- Each of us is uniquely designed and shaped by God to do certain things. Find your shape and use it to serve Him.[4]

We all have the corporate calling to spread the good news of salvation around the world.

---

[4] Rick Warren: The Purpose Driven Life page 249 till 255

SHAPE

a) **S**piritual Gifts. (I Cor. 12, Rom. 8, Eph. 4). Your spiritual gifts reveal a part of God's will for your ministry, but not all of it.

b) **H**eart. Passion, this represents the centre of your motivation, desires, interests, and inclinations, why you say the things you do (Matt. 12:34), why you feel the way you do (Psalm 37:4), and why you act the way you do. (Prov. 4:23)

c) **A**bilities. These are the natural talents that you were born with. The average person possesses from 500-700 skills. The real issues:

- People need some process of skill identification
- People need a process to help them match their abilities to the right ministry

d) **P**ersonality. There is no right or wrong temperament for ministry; all kinds of personalities are needed to balance the church. Your personality affects how you use your gifts and abilities. When members' minister in a manner that is consistent with their personalities, they enjoy fulfilment, satisfaction and fruitfulness.

e) **E**xperiences. God never wastes an experience (Rom 8:28), be it educational, vocational, spiritual, ministry, and painful.

Instead of trying to reshape yourself to be like someone else, celebrate the SHAPE God has given you. You will be most effective and fulfilled in ministry when you use your abilities in the area of your gifting.

DISCOVERING YOUR SPIRITUAL GIFTS

Are you interested in finding your spiritual gifts so you can yield to your calling and serve effectively in your local Church? Take the Wagner test attached to the tail of this book. (Appendix 4) [5]

The test has been so helpful in our various Church training.

This guide to discovering your spiritual gifts should not be viewed as a test. The only right answers here are honest answers.

The answers you provide will help you find your areas of strength within the realm of Christian service.[6]

> Your being a Son of God is as real as your being alive. It doesn't depend on your thoughts or feelings but on the unbreakable word of God.
> As you daily nourish your spirit man with the word of God, all areas of your life will be aligned with the expectation of God concerning you.

TAKING YOUR PLACE IN YOUR GENERATION

But you are not like that, for you are a chosen people. You are royal priests, a holy nation, and God's very own possession. As a result, you can show others the goodness of God, for he called you out of the darkness into his wonderful light. **1 Peter 2:9**

1) **The world is one family of God's creation (Psalm 24:1)**

Our economies and relationships are more interdependent and interlinked than ever through information technology and advancements

---

[5] Take a Wagner test (freely available freely on the internet and)attached to the end of this book as Appendix 4
[6] Ditto

in international transportation. The food and clothes and products you use are from all the parts of the world now.

It is now a matter of economics and demand and supply that determine where your products come from. As a global citizen and ambassador, you are expected to touch the world more than the previous generations that did not have the same technological advantage that we have now.

2) **You are God's tool to save the world**

a) Believers are created to be solution providers ("Christ in you, the hope of glory" **Col 1:27).** There is no limit to our potentials to make our world a glorious place (Eph. 3:20.) No way of exhausting the supply of ideas leading to fresh discoveries, and inventions. More ideas, more discoveries and innovation, we birth. The more we invent, the more we prosper and the more we convert new ideas to inventions.

b) You don't need to quit your work and become a full-time missionary or evangelist to make this impact on someone's life. In fact, your profession and closeness in the office offer you access to some people no full-time evangelist can reach. There are people around you, that given your education, closeness and relationship you are the best person that can lead them to Christ. Don't limit yourself. Don't fail them! Don't fail God. Save their lives!

- As a global citizen, you can affect the world through the followings:

a) **Save souls**. That was, in fact, the last commission Jesus Christ gave His disciples before His ascension to heaven (Matt. 28:19). The only way to invest your wealth in heaven is to invest it while on earth in saving souls that will be with you in heaven eternally. That is the only way to convert earthly wealth to eternal wealth.

Let your heart focus on the eternal things of the Lord rather than the perishing thing on this earth. For where your treasure is, there your heart will be also. (Matt.6:21)

b) **Offering prayers**. Prayer affects all things, and we can now all be globally involved in any activity in the world. Ask me, and I will make the nations your inheritance, the ends of the earth your possession Psalm 2:8. Pray for pastors and missionaries all over the world. Pray for believers that are being victimized by terrorists and violent people.

c) **Media and Public Protest**. Governments are easily affected by public opinions on the internet and social media nowadays. Make your voice heard all over the world as a follower of Christ. Join other believers who are protesting against corruption and bad government.

d) **Resist believers' discrimination and oppression all over the world**. Many nations under the surge of humanism are removing the Bible out of schools. Resist these negative developments by making your voice heard.

e) **Internet evangelism**. We can all send flyers; preach messages, forward vital information for Church growth now through the internet, emails and social media. It is very easy to be an evangelist nowadays and reach many souls daily with little efforts. We have all been given the great commission to go all over the world to share the good tidings of the gospel. Only internet and other information technology have made that commission easier to obey.

f) **Finance gospel.** Most importantly, if you are too busy to travel around the world and still too busy to maximize internet technology to save souls, you can at least invest in your Church and other godly ministries doing it. I do not mean paying tithes or offering, which is a basic responsibility expected of every believer. You should be regularly investing your money in the purpose of the Lord. Your priority should be building the kingdom of God.

3) **The church is your training school**

- The Church offers you courses while the world offers you the field to practice the word of God. The ultimate duty of every Christian is to be a soul winner in the marketplace.

4) **The world at large is your working place**

a) We have been blessed to multiply and replenish the earth (Gen. 1:28.)

I. Multiply: This is an instruction to increase and reproduce more of your fruits in quality and quantity.

- Emphasis: Earn multiple incomes with your (ageless) gifts: For example, you can teach language, sew clothe and sell food items in addition to your normal job.

II. Replenish: This means to make full or to fill again.

- Emphasis: Believers are called to reverse the destructive work of the enemy. We are to fill or make complete again the earth.

b) The original plan for man is to fill the earth with God's glory. We are here to fulfil an assignment of restoring God's glory to the earth

Christianity is more than:

- Salvation and praising the Lord
- It is not just about your healing and blessing etc.
- It is more than just serving the Lord as Church workers
- It's about God filling the earth with His glory through believers!

5) **Every work is a sacred service to the Lord**

The Catholic Church in the past has misled people by differentiating between sacred (spiritual) and secular (worldly, temporal) works.

a) We are all ambassadors of Christ with a mandate to restore mankind to the Lord (2 Cor. 5:17-20; Eph. 6:10-15.)

b) We are all called (from the pulpit and the pew) to evangelize the world. The marketplace is the pulpit for every believer.

As Christ ambassadors, we are to cover every societal pillar (Deut. 7:1):

- Government/politics;
- Economy/Business;
- Education; Family;
- Religion & Culture;
- Arts, Entertainment & sports,
- Media and communication,
- Transportation, Information technology, etc.

c) We have the promise of God to back us up in our kingdom service.

Behold, I have given you authority to tread on serpents and scorpions, and over all the power of the enemy, and nothing shall hurt you **Luke 10:19**

And these signs shall follow them that believe; In my name shall they cast out devils; they shall speak with new tongues; 18 They shall take up serpents; and if they drink any deadly thing, it shall not hurt them; they shall lay hands on the sick, and they shall recover **Mark 16:17-18**

"And Jesus came and spake unto them, saying, All power is given unto me in heaven and in earth. Go ye therefore, and teach all nations, baptizing them in the name of the Father, and of the Son, and of the Holy Ghost: Teaching them to observe all things whatsoever I have commanded you: and, lo, I am with you alway, even unto the end of the world. Amen" **Matthew 28:18-20**

Called and anointed to be fruitful

Our corporate mission on earth as sons of God and followers of Jesus Christ is to conduct a spiritual mission that is capable of filling the earth with the gospel of Christ (gospel globalization).

Jesus' Church is a "Go Ye Church, not a Sit Thee Church."

Our calling is to be a global Church, not a local one!

> **As a global citizen and ambassador, you are expected to touch the world more than the previous generations that did not have the same technological advantage that we have now.**

PRAYER POINTS

Verily I say unto you, Whatsoever ye shall bind on earth shall be bound in heaven: and whatsoever ye shall loose on earth shall be loosed in heaven. 19 Again I say unto you, That if two of you shall agree on earth as touching anything that they shall ask, it shall be done for them of my Father which is in heaven. **Matt 18:18-19**

1. In the Name of Jesus, I revoke and negate every death sentence in my life, my Church and in my community. (Psalm 118:17)
2. I declare that I overcome the enemy by the Blood of the Lamb and the word of my testimony. (Rev. 12:11)
3. Heavenly Father, bless me with a spiritual gift that will distinguish my life forever in your service. (1 Cor. 15:57)
4. Let everything in me contradicting the word of God; submit to the leading of the Holy Spirit today. Amen. (2 Cor. 10:5)
5. Lord Jesus Christ, let your presence overshadow me and let the Holy Spirit empower me for all round victories. (Deut. 20:1-4)
6. I declare that I will not die before my time. I will live to declare the glory of the Lord in the land of the living. (Psalm 20:7-8; 118:17)
7. Heavenly Father, cause your favour to enthrone me and make me your voice into my generation. (Psalm 91:16)

**We are all called (from the pulpit and the pew) to evangelize the world.
The market place is the pulpit for every believer.**

CHAPTER 7: KEYS TO SUCCESSFUL EXISTENCE

Keep this Book of the Law always on your lips; meditate on it day and night, so that you may be careful to do everything written in it. Then you will be prosperous and successful. **Josh 1:8 (NIV)**

Many enrol in classes with success experts and inspirational speakers at the onset of every year in order to enjoy a successful year. However, the Bible teaches us that it is the only compendium of success. Success is in this book! Study this Book of Instruction continually (Psalm 1:1-3) and apply it to your life. Only then will you prosper and succeed in all you do.

THE PRINCIPLES OF SUCCESS

1. Success is the completion and fulfilment of the original purpose of a product

- Your success is about fulfilling the reason for your existence. It is not about making big money, assets, even living longer. Rather, it is about the discovery and fulfilment of your purpose.
- Your enduring action determines the longevity of your success (endurance ensures success).

2. The purpose of a thing is decided by the manufacturer, not by the customer or the sales force

- The purpose is discovered not decided by product. Your purpose is decided by God.

3. Success is inbuilt to every product by manufacturers

Every company tests, product (iPad, car, tyres, etc. before selling it.) The ability to fulfil its purpose is inbuilt by a manufacturer into his product. An average car, for instance, is built to speed till 220Km/hour.

a) **Life is designed by God to be successful**
- *An unadulterated seed will always bring tree. Fish will always swim. Pregnancy will always turn into a baby.*

b) **Nothing God created is meant to fail.**
- *Before I formed you in the womb, I knew you before you were born, I set you apart; I appointed you as a prophet to the nations.* **Jer. 1:5**
- *Your eyes saw my unformed body; all the days ordained for me were written in your book before one of them came to be.* **Ps. 139:16 (14-18)**

4. The success of a product is important for the manufacturer
- *Birds fly naturally, fish swim naturally, seeds grow naturally all to their best. Success is natural for every obedient child of God.* **Isa 1:19**
- *Whatever He called you to do, you have the inbuilt ability.* **1 Thess. 5:24**

5. There is no failure in God's plan for you

For I know the thoughts that I think toward you, saith the LORD, thoughts of peace, and not of evil, to give you an expected end. **Jer. 29:11**

- Failure is not meant to halt your success, but rather to provoke you to success.
- Every failure has come to pull you towards your purpose. All things shall work together. **Rom. 8:28**

6. Success is designed by God to be predictable (just like a failure) Psalm 1:1-3
- Life success is predictably attached to the operation of principles (order). Ps 1:1-3
- God of purpose is God of standard &principles. Life of success and failure are predictable

I. **Ignorance of principles has painful repercussion. Hosea 4:6**
- Ignorance of the law is no excuse to break it. For instance, if you ignorantly break the law of gravity, it will break you.

II. **Wrong application, abuse or misuse has its punishment.**
- Failure to apply principles correctly leads to failure in life. Many do not succeed because they only pray instead of applying principles of success into their lives (in addition to their prayers.)

III. **Disobedience to law negates the prayer force. Deut. 28:15-68**
- God's purpose requires our cooperation to accomplish since we are consciously created, as creatures of free will.
- God is sovereign, and you are responsible. That is the basic principles of the Bible (Isaiah 1:19.)

7. Success is a product of timely pursuits

Time was created by God for man on earth. In heaven and eternity, there is no time, but on earth, everything is about time.

For every purpose, there is a time (Eccl.3:1).

8. You are solely responsible for your success through choice and decisions you make (Josh. 1:8)

Blessed is the man that walketh not in the counsel of the ungodly, nor standeth in the way of sinners, nor sitteth in the seat of the scornful. 2 But his delight is in the law of the Lord; and in his law doth he meditate day and night. 3 And he shall be like a tree planted by the rivers of water, that bringeth forth his fruit in his season; his leaf also shall not wither; and whatsoever he doeth shall prosper. **Psalm 1:1-3**

a) Success is a game of endurance (Hab. 2:1-3).

b) Only those who can endure to the end can be successful.

Many are the plans in a person's heart, but it is the LORD's purpose that prevails. Refuse to give up on your pursuits of destiny and purpose.

Stop associating with those going nowhere. You should not be associating with evil doers if you want God to be your Guide.

THE PLACE OF ASSOCIATION AND APPRECIATION IN THE FULFILMENT OF PURPOSE

Do not be misled: "Bad company corrupts good character." **1 Cor. 15:33** *(NIV)*

He that walketh with wise men shall be wise: but a companion of fools shall be destroyed. **Proverbs 13:20**

Show me your friends and associates, and I can predict your future.

That is because your associates do not just mirror what you appreciate; they serve to affirm your values, mindsets and lifestyles.

Appreciation is the destination of associates of the wise while destruction is the final station for friends of fools.

A researcher once found out that an average person earns the average salary of his three best friends. That is how deep we are affected by the company we keep. I have seen people with great potentials and future derailed and destroyed for wrong friendship and fellowship.

So long we are alive; we will all have challenges and tribulations.

Who are your counsellors who advise you when you have a problem?

That will determine if your challenges will demote or promote you.

Over and over, it is proven that we tend to move towards the people we admire and copy their lifestyles. Many of our youths are corrupt and misguided because their social role models are emotionally bankrupt and have no social value to teach them. Watch out for those that your kid cherishes. Whoever you admire affects your life values greatly.

> **Life success is predictably attached to the operation of principles (Psalm 1:1-3)**

Appreciation

Your attitude determines your altitude.

Your attitude of gratitude determines your altitude in life.

Nothing depreciates a man like a lack of gratitude.

No one cherishes ingrates. Your lifestyle is a direct product of your mindset. A lazy hearted man will continue to procrastinate while a boisterous and passionate man will not cease from labour till he secures his rewards. The reason many do not appreciate is that they compare themselves to others. Comparison is a game of losers. The truth is that no one is created to be a copy of another. We are all different and original to the core, and our relevance and values are hidden in our difference. The best way to climb up in life is to apply winning principles (noticed in the lives of other people) into your life.

You need to only compare yourself to yourself in terms of maturity and productivity. If you are getting better, you are appreciating, and when your performance is going backwards, you are depreciating. Appreciate what pulls you forward and devote your time to increase in it.

Association

Nothing leverages a man ahead like making the opportunity of other people's experience, ability and knowledge. Isaac Newton was known to say, "If I see farther, it is because I stand on the shoulders of giants." There are some associations that when you miss, will make you a loser forever. Lot missed his winning edge when he lost contact with His uncle, Abraham. You can suffer a significant loss in life or excel in your pursuits extraordinarily depending on the company you keep.

Most people who have criminal tendencies acquire, such as a result of growing up in bad environments with improper associates.

The bad associate is one of the most common causes of failure in business. In marketing personal services, make it a serious duty to pick people who are worthy of emulation.

We emulate those with whom we associate most closely with.

Get yourself together

Stop blaming people or circumstances for your situation.

Take a look at a mirror, and as soon as you see your face, poke a finger at him and chant, "guilty, guilty, and guilty!"

Yes, for every situation, you have yourself to blame or to praise.

You are simply responsible for the association you keep, the appreciation you give and the admiration you secure from other people.

The association you cherish is determined by the values you appreciate in life, and the values you appreciate in life are determined by your personal taste. If you don't like your associates, change your lifestyles and if you don't like your lifestyle, change your mindsets.

Life is what you make it. You can have it the way you like.

And you will have yourself to like or hate for the result you get.

Want to live right in the future? Then prepare right for it today.

Think right, choose right and do it right, today!

Your success is about fulfilling the reason for your existence. It is not about making big money… Rather, it is about the discovery and fulfilment of your purpose.

PRAYER POINTS

Blessed is the man that walketh not in the counsel of the ungodly, nor standeth in the way of sinners, nor sitteth in the seat of the scornful. 2 But his delight is in the law of the LORD; and in his law doth he meditate day and night. 3 And he shall be like a tree planted by the rivers of water, that bringeth forth his fruit in his season; his leaf also shall not wither; and whatsoever he doeth shall prosper. **Ps. 1:1-3**

1. May the Blood of Jesus speak victory into my life and silent every accusation of the enemy against my life in Jesus mighty name. (Revelation 12:11)

2. Dear Holy Spirit, empower me to serve the LORD, all the days of my life. (Psalm 118:17; 1 Cor. 12:27)

3. I declare that I will walk in health and strength all the days of my life. I will accomplish everything God has assigned to me to do with excellence and distinction. (3 John 1:2)

4. Heavenly Father, cause whatever I do to prosper and let me bear fruit even in my old age. (Psalm 92:14)

5. Holy Spirit, help me to remain rooted in my faith in the Lord and in my fellowship with His body. (1 Cor. 12:27)

6. Father, my Lord, direct my helpers to me, anywhere they may be, in the name of Jesus. May I live long to enjoy the blessings and the goodness of the LORD in the land of the living.

7. I will serve the LORD all the days of my life. (Psalm 118:17)

APPENDIXES

APPENDIX 1: DISCOVERING YOUR POTENTIAL TEST

I praise you because I am fearfully and wonderfully made; your works are wonderful, I know that full well. **Psalm 139:14 (NIV)**

1. **What is potential? Give two explanations of what potential is.**
a)

b)

2. **List 8 out of the 12 principles of potential**
a)

b)

c)

d)

e)

f)

g)

h)

3. **Five major ways of discovering and developing your potential are all listed below. Explain them in your own words.**

a) Recognize and celebrate your difference.

b) Take hold of your dream and vision.

c) Study to develop your potentials.

d) Develop human relationship and networks (Soft skills).

e) Pursue your purpose with obsession.

APPENDIX 2: DISCOVERING YOUR DESTINY TEST

The days of our years are threescore years and ten; and if by reason of strength they be fourscore years, yet is their strength labour and sorrow; for it is soon cut off, and we fly away. **Psalm 90:10**

Life is not just about growing old; it is about living fulfilled to the extent that you can say, like Jesus Christ that, "It is finished."

Jesus died at a young age of 33, and we are still under the impacts of His three and a half years of ministry. Will your life make an impact too? That depends on if you are able to fulfil your destiny too.

1) What are the five means of locating your destiny?

a)

b)

c)

d)

e)

2) State 4 or 5 major steps to fulfil your destiny

a)

b)

c)

d)

e)

APPENDIX 3: DISCOVERING YOUR PURPOSE TEST

In whom also we have obtained an inheritance, being predestinated according to the purpose of him who worketh all things after the counsel of his own will. **Eph. 1:11**

You need to locate your purpose before you can fulfil it.
Preparation, however, precedes the fulfilment of purpose.
Answer now, the following:

a) Purpose is discovered, not self-determined. Explain

b) What are the 7 major questions to help you locate and fulfil your purpose in life?

I.

II.

III.

IV.

V.

VI.

VII.

3) Destiny is a personal purpose and purpose is public destiny. Explain

4) Discovery of purpose helps you to determine your potentials. Explain.

APPENDIX 4: WAGNER SPIRITUAL TEST

Before You Start

Follow These Four Steps:

Step 1 - Print out the answer sheet from the next page. Go through the list of 125 statements on the questionnaire in part four. For each one, mark on the answer sheet to what extent the statement is true of your life: **MUCH = 3, SOME = 2, LITTLE = 1, or NOT AT ALL = 0.**

Warning! Do not score according to what you think should be true or hope might be true in the future. Be honest and score on the basis of past experience. If you are a young Christian or new in the faith, the results will need extra care in interpretation.

Step 2 - When you are finished, score the questionnaire according to the instructions on the scoring sheet.

Step 3 - Study the gift definitions and Scripture references.

Step 4 - Complete the exercises to gain a tentative evaluation of your gifts and explore the implications for your ministry in the Body of Christ.

Instructions for Scoring

Turn to your Score Sheet.

Now, add your Score Sheet answers together, from left to right, and write that total in the Totals box next to each gift.

Example: Add together the number you wrote in box 1, plus the number in box 26, plus the number in box 51, plus the number in box 76 and the number in box 101. Those five numbers added together, become your total score to be written in the Totals box.

Directions

When you have finished responding to all 125 statements and are ready to score your test, follow the instructions listed. When your Score Sheet is totalled, return to this page for further instructions.

STEP 1

After adding up your points, you should have several, notably high scores. These are your probable spiritual gifts. Please indicate them below, starting with your highest score. Any score below 12, however, is probably not a positive indicator of a gift. If you had other high scores, or if you feel sure you have certain gifts even though they didn't receive high marks, put them down as well.

You have just taken the first step toward discovering your spiritual gifts. Please understand that this exercise only indicates your probable gifts. Over the next few weeks, you should use the following five steps to more clearly determine your spiritual gifts.

STEP 2

Pray, believing that God will continue to reveal to you what gifts He has given you. Don't forget 1 Cor. 12:11: Gifts have been distributed "to each individual." Pray also for the wisdom and desire to use your gifts with greater efficiency for Him.

STEP 3

Study the Bible passages that deal specifically with this topic: Romans 12, 1 Corinthians 12-14, Ephesians 3, 4 and 1 Peter 4. And take the time to reflect on the contexts of the many Bible stories of men and women who used their gifts for God. Such accounts serve as examples and as inspiration.

STEP 4

Experiment by using your new-found gifts. This may be a new experience, and you may not know where to start. See the next page for some suggestions. As you begin to work for God, your gifts will develop in an exciting way.

STEP 5

Confirm the gifts of others. When you see another person using his gift effectively, say so. This isn't flattery; it's a vital step in the ongoing process of spiritual gift development.

Let's begin this process right away. Please mark down the spiritual gifts you've observed in three fellow Christians in your congregation. Your keen observations will be appreciated by each of them and your pastor.

This is a good opportunity to let your friends know what their gifts are, simply by listing them here. It's also a good time to let them know, in a very gracious (and anonymous) way, what their gifts aren't by leaving those gifts off the list. Make this an honest appraisal.

The summary of gifts beginning on the next page may help you in your evaluation.

STEP 6

Expect confirmation of your gifts by other church members. Following your handing in this inventory to your pastor, your inventory will be returned listing some of the gifts your fellow believers have observed in you. Everyone who hands in his inventory should receive an evaluation. You may not agree with this evaluation! But instead of dismissing these opinions, explore them. Look for ways to develop the abilities.

WAGNER-MODIFIED HOUTS ANSWER SHEET

ROWS	VALUE OF ANSWERS					TOTAL	GIFT
A	1	26	51	76	101		
B	2	27	52	77	102		
C	3	28	53	78	103		
D	4	29	54	79	104		
E	5	30	55	80	105		
F	6	31	56	81	106		
G	7	32	57	82	107		
H	8	33	58	83	108		
I	9	34	59	84	109		
J	10	35	60	85	110		
K	11	36	61	86	111		
L	12	37	62	87	112		
M	13	38	63	88	113		
N	14	39	64	89	114		
O	15	40	65	90	115		
P	16	41	66	91	116		
Q	17	42	67	92	117		

ROWS	VALUE OF ANSWERS					TOTAL	GIFT
R	18	43	68	93	118		
S	19	44	69	94	119		
T	20	45	70	95	120		
U	21	46	71	96	121		
V	22	47	72	97	122		
W	23	48	73	98	123		
X	24	49	74	99	124		
Y	25	50	75	100	125		

WAGNER-MODIFIED HOUTS QUESTIONNAIRE

For each statement, mark to what extent it is true of your life: MUCH = 3, SOME = 2, LITTLE = 1, or NOT AT ALL = 0.

1. I have a desire to speak direct messages from God that edify, exhort or comfort others.
2. I have enjoyed relating to a certain group of people over a long period of time, sharing personally in their successes and their failures.
3. People have told me that I have helped them learn the biblical truth in meaningful ways.
4. I have applied spiritual truth effectively to situations in my own life.
5. Others have told me I have helped them distinguish key and important facts of Scripture.
6. I have verbally encouraged the wavering, the troubled or the discouraged.

7. Others in the church have noted that I have been able to see through phoniness before it was evident to other people.
8. I find I manage money well in order to give liberally to the Lord's work.
9. I have assisted Christian leaders to relieve them for their essential job.
10. I have a desire to work with those who have physical or mental problems, to alleviate their suffering.
11. I feel comfortable relating to ethnics and minorities, and they seem to accept me.
12. I have led others to a decision for salvation through faith in Christ.
13. My home is always open to people passing through who need a place to stay.
14. When in a group, I am the one others often look to for vision and direction.
15. When I speak, people seem to listen and agree.
16. When a group I am in is lacking organisation, I step in to fill the gap.
17. Others can point to specific instances where my prayers have resulted in visible miracles.
18. In the name of the Lord, I have been used in curing diseases instantaneously.
19. I have spoken in tongues.
20. Sometimes when a person speaks in tongues, I get an idea about what God is saying.
21. I could live more comfortably, but I choose not to in order to live with the poor.
22. I am single and enjoy it.
23. I spend at least an hour a day in prayer.
24. I have spoken to evil spirits, and they have obeyed me.
25. I enjoy being called upon to do special jobs around the church.
26. Through God, I have revealed specific things that will happen in the future.
27. I have enjoyed assuming the responsibility for the spiritual well-being of a particular group of Christians.

28. I feel I can explain the New Testament teaching about the health and ministry of the Body of Christ in a relevant way.
29. I can intuitively arrive at solutions to fairly complicated problems.
30. I have had insights of spiritual truth that others have said helped bring them closer to God.
31. I can effectively motivate people to get involved in ministry when it is needed.
32. I can "see" the Spirit of God resting on certain people from time to time.
33. My giving records show that I give considerably more than 10 per cent of my income to the Lord's work.
34. Other people have told me that I have helped them become more effective in their ministries.
35. I have cared for others when they have had material or physical needs.
36. I feel I could learn another language well in order to minister to those in a different culture.
37. I have shared joyfully how Christ has brought me to Himself in a way that is meaningful to non-believers.
38. I enjoy taking charge of church suppers or social events.
39. I have believed God for the impossible and seen it happen in a tangible way.
40. Other Christians have followed my leadership because they believed in me.
41. I enjoy handling the details of organising ideas, people, resources and time for more effective ministry.
42. God has used me personally to perform supernatural signs and wonders.
43. I enjoy praying for sick people because I know that many of them will be healed as a result.
44. I have spoken an immediate message of God to His people in a language I have never learned.
45. I have interpreted tongues with the result that the Body of Christ was edified, exhorted or comforted.

46. Living a simple lifestyle is an exciting challenge for me.
47. Other people have noted that I feel more indifferent about not being married than most.
48. When I hear a prayer request, I pray for that need for several days at least.
49. I have actually heard a demon speak in a loud voice.
50. I don't have many special skills, but I do what needs to be done around the church.
51. People have told me that I have communicated timely and urgent messages that must have come directly from the Lord.
52. I feel unafraid of giving spiritual guidance and direction in a group of Christians.
53. I can devote considerable time to learning new biblical truths in order to communicate them to others.
54. When a person has a problem, I can frequently guide him or her to the best biblical solution.
55. Through study or experience, I have discerned major strategies or techniques God seems to use in furthering His kingdom.
56. People have come to me in their afflictions or suffering and told me that they have been helped, relieved and healed.
57. I can tell with a fairly high degree of assurance when a person is afflicted by an evil spirit.
58. When I am moved by an appeal to give to God's work, I usually can find the money I need to do it.
59. I have enjoyed doing routine tasks that have led to a more effective ministry by others.
60. I enjoy visiting in hospitals and/or retirement homes and feel I do well in such a ministry.
61. People of a different race or culture have been attracted to me, and we have related well.
62. Non-Christians have noted that they feel comfortable when they are around me and that I have a positive effect on them toward developing faith in Christ.

63. When people come to our home, they indicate that they "feel at home" with us.
64. Other people have told me that I had faith to accomplish what seemed impossible to them.
65. When I set goals, others seem to accept them readily.
66. I have been able to make effective and efficient plans for accomplishing the goals of a group.
67. God regularly seems to do impossible things through my life.
68. Others have told me that God healed them of emotional problems when I ministered to them.
69. I can speak to God in a language I have never learned.
70. I have prayed that I may interpret if someone begins speaking in tongues.
71. I am not poor, but I can identify with poor people.
72. I am glad I have more time to serve the Lord because I am single.
73. Intercessory prayer is one of my favourite ways of spending time.
74. Others call on me when they suspect that someone is demonised.
75. Others have mentioned that I seem to enjoy routine tasks and do well at them.
76. I sometimes have a strong sense of what God wants to say to people in response to particular situations.
77. I have helped fellow believers by guiding them to relevant portions of the Bible and praying with them.
78. I feel I can communicate biblical truths to others and see resulting changes in knowledge, attitudes, values or conduct.
79. Some people indicate that I have perceived and applied biblical truth to the specific needs of fellow believers.
80. I study and read quite a bit in order to learn new biblical truths.
81. I have a desire to effectively counsel the perplexed, the guilty or the addicted.
82. I can recognise whether a person's teaching is from God, from Satan, or of human origin.
83. I am so confident that God will meet my needs that I give to Him sacrificially and consistently.

84. When I do things behind the scenes and others are helped, I am joyful.
85. People call on me to help those who are less fortunate.
86. I would be willing to leave comfortable surroundings if it would enable me to share Christ with more people.
87. I get frustrated when others don't seem to share their faith with unbelievers as much as I do.
88. Others have mentioned to me that I am a very hospitable person.
89. There have been times when I have felt sure I knew God's specific will for the future growth of His work, even when others are not so sure.
90. When I join a group, others seem to back off and expect me to take the lead.
91. I am able to give directions to others without using persuasion to get them to accomplish tasks.
92. People have told me that I was God's instrument which brought supernatural change in lives or circumstances.
93. I have prayed for others and physical healing has actually occurred.
94. When I give a public message in tongues, I expect it to be interpreted.
95. I have interpreted tongues in a way that seemed to bless others.
96. Others tell me I sacrifice much materially in order to minister.
97. I am single and have little difficulty controlling my sexual desires.
98. Others have told me that my prayers for them have been answered in tangible ways.
99. Other people have been instantly delivered from demonic oppression when I have prayed.
100. I prefer being active and doing something rather than just sitting around talking, reading or listening to a speaker.
101. I sometimes feel that I know exactly what God wants to do in ministry at a specific point in time.
102. People have told me that I have helped them be restored to the Christian community.

103. Studying the Bible and sharing my insights with others is very satisfying for me.
104. I have felt an unusual presence of God and personal confidence when important decisions needed to be made.
105. I have the ability to discover new truths for myself through reading or observing situations firsthand.
106. I have urged others to seek biblical solutions to their affliction or suffering.
107. I can tell whether a person speaking in tongues is genuine.
108. I have been willing to maintain a lower standard of living in order to benefit God's work.
109. When I serve the Lord, I really don't care who gets the credit.
110. I would enjoy spending time with a lonely, shut-in person or someone in prison.
111. More than most, I have had a strong desire to see peoples of other countries won to the Lord.
112. I am attracted to non-believers because of my desire to win them to Christ.
113. I have desired to make my home available to those in the Lord's service whenever needed.
114. Others have told me that I am a person of unusual vision, and I agree.
115. When I am in charge, things seem to run smoothly.
116. I have enjoyed bearing the responsibility for the success of a particular task within my church.
117. In the name of the Lord, I have been able to recover sight to the blind.

118. When I pray for the sick, either I or they feel sensations of tingling or warmth.
119. When I speak in tongues, I believe it is edifying to the Lord's Body.
120. I have interpreted tongues in such a way that the message appeared to be directly from God.
121. Poor people accept me because I choose to live on their level.

122. I readily identify with Paul's desire for others to be single as he was.
123. When I pray, God frequently speaks to me, and I recognise His voice.
124. I cast out demons in Jesus' name.
125. I respond cheerfully when asked to do a job, even if it seems menial.

Gift Definitions and Scripture References

A. Prophecy. The gift of prophecy is the special ability that God gives to certain members of the Body of Christ to receive and communicate an immediate message of God to His people through a divinely anointed utterance.
Luke 7:26 - Acts 15:32 - Acts 21:9-11 - Romans 12:6 - I Corinthians 12:10, 28 - Ephesians 4:11-14

B. Pastor. The gift of pastor is the special ability that God gives to certain members of the Body of Christ to assume long-term personal responsibility for the spiritual welfare of a group of believers.
John 10:1-18 - Ephesians 4:11-14 - I Timothy 3:1-7 - I Peter 5:1-3

C. Teaching. The gift of teaching is the special ability that God gives to certain members of the Body of Christ to communicate information relevant to the health and ministry of the Body and its members in such a way that others will learn.
Acts 18:24-28 - Acts 20:20,21 - Romans 12:71 - Corinthians 12:28 - Ephesians 4:11-14

D. Wisdom. The gift of wisdom is the special ability that God gives to certain members of the Body of Christ to know the mind of the Holy Spirit in such a way as to receive insight into how given knowledge may best be applied to specific needs arising in the Body of Christ.
Acts 6:3,10 - I Cor. 2:1-13 - I Cor. 12:8 - James 1:5,6 - 2 Peter 3:15,16

E. Knowledge. The gift of knowledge is the special ability that God gives to certain members of the Body of Christ to discover, accumulate, analyse and clarify information and ideas which are pertinent to the well-being of the Body.
Acts 5:1-11 - I Cor. 2:14 - 1 Cor. 12:8 - 2 Cor. 11:6 - Col. 2:2,3

F. Exhortation. The gift of exhortation is the special ability that God gives to certain members of the Body of Christ to minister words of comfort, consolation, encouragement and counsel to other members of the Body in such a way that they feel helped and healed.
Acts 14:22 - Romans 12:8 - 1 Timothy 4:13 - Hebrews 10:25

G. Discerning of Spirits. The gift of discerning of spirits is the special ability that God gives to certain members of the Body of Christ to know with assurance whether certain behaviour purported to be of God is in reality divine, human or Satanic.
Matt. 16:21-23 - Acts 5:1-11 - Acts 16:16-18 - 1 Cor. 12:10 - I John 4:1-6

H. Giving. The gift of giving is the special ability that God gives to certain members of the Body of Christ to contribute their material resources to the work of the Lord with liberality and cheerfulness.
Mark 12:41-44 - Romans 12:8 - 2 Corinthians 8:1-7 - 2 Corinthians 9:2-8

I. Helps. The gift of help is the special ability that God gives to certain members of the Body of Christ to invest the talents they have in the life and ministry of other members of the Body, thus enabling those others to increase the effectiveness of their own spiritual gifts.
Mark 15:40,41 - Luke 8:2,3 - Acts 9:36 - Romans 16:1,2 - 1 Cor. 12:28

J. Mercy. The gift of mercy is the special ability that God gives to certain members of the Body of Christ to feel genuine empathy and compassion for individuals (both Christian and non-Christian) who suffer distressing physical, mental or emotional problems, and to translate that compassion into cheerfully done deeds which reflect Christ's love and alleviate the suffering.
Matthew 20:29-34 - Matthew 25:34-40 - Mark 9:41 - Luke 10:33-35 - Acts 11:28-30 - Acts 16:33,34 - Romans 12:8

K. Missionary. The gift of missionary is the special ability that God gives to certain members of the Body of Christ to minister whatever other spiritual gifts they have in a second culture.
Acts 8:4 - Acts 13:2,3 - Acts 22:21 - Romans 10:15 - 1 Cor. 9:19-23

L. Evangelist. The gift of evangelist is the special ability that God gives to certain members of the Body of Christ to share the gospel with unbelievers in such a way that men and women become Jesus' disciples and responsible members of the Body of Christ.
Acts 8:5,6 - Acts 8:26-40 - Acts 14:21 - Acts 21:8 - Ephesians 4:11-14 - 2 Timothy 4:5

M. Hospitality. The gift of hospitality is the special ability that God gives to certain members of the Body of Christ to provide an open house and a warm welcome to those in need of food and lodging.
Acts 16:14,15 - Romans 12:9-13 - Romans 16:23 - Hebrews 13:1,2 - 1 Peter 4:9

N. Faith. The gift of faith is the special ability that God gives to certain members of the Body of Christ to discern with extraordinary confidence the will and purposes of God for his work..
Acts 11:22-24 - Acts 27:21-25 - Romans 4:18-21 - 1 Corinthians 12:9 - Hebrews 11

0. Leadership. The gift of leadership is the special ability that God gives to certain members of the Body of Christ to set goals in accordance with God's purpose for the future and to communicate these goals to others in such a way that they voluntarily and harmoniously work together to accomplish those goals for the glory of God.
Lk. 9:51 - Acts 7:10 - Acts 15:7-11 - Rom.12:8 - 1Tim. S:17 - Heb. 13:17

P. Administration. The gift of administration is the special ability that God gives to certain members of the Body of Christ to understand clearly the immediate and long-range goals of a particular unit of the Body of Christ and to devise and execute effective plans for the accomplishment of those goals.
Luke 14:28-30 - Acts 6:1-7 - Acts 27:11 - 1 Corinthians 12:28 - Titus 1:5

Q. Miracles. The gift of miracles is the special ability that God gives to certain members of the Body of Christ to serve as human intermediaries through whom it pleases God to perform powerful acts that are perceived by observers to have altered the ordinary course of nature.
Acts 9:36-42 - Acts 19:11-20 - Acts 20:7-12 - Romans 15:18,19 - 1 Corinthians 12:10,28 - 2 Corinthians 12:12

R. Healing. The gift of healing is the special ability that God gives to certain members of the Body of Christ to serve as human intermediaries through whom it pleases God to cure illness and restore health apart from the use of natural means.
Acts 3:1-10 - Acts 5:12-16 - Acts 9:32-35 - Acts 28:7-10 - 1 Corinthians 12:9,28

S. Tongues. The gift of tongues is the special ability that God gives to certain members of the Body of Christ (a) to speak to God in a language they have never learned and/or (b) to receive and communicate an immediate message of God to his people through a divinely anointed utterance in a language they never learned.
Mark 16:17 - Acts 2:1-13 - Acts 10:44-46 - Acts 19:1-7 - 1 Corinthians 12:10,28 - 1 Corinthians 14:13-19

T. Interpretation. The gift of interpretation is the special ability that God gives to certain members of the Body of Christ to make known in the vernacular the message of one who speaks in tongues.
1 Corinthians 12:10,30 - 1 Corinthians 14:13 - 1 Corinthians 14:26-28

U. Voluntary Poverty. The gift of voluntary poverty is the special ability that God gives to certain members of the Body of Christ to renounce material comfort and luxury and adopt a personal lifestyle equivalent to those living at the poverty level in a given society in order to serve God more effectively.
Acts 2:44,45 - Acts 4:34-37 - 1 Cor. 13:1-3 - 2 Cor. 6:10 - 2 Cor. 8:9

V. Celibacy. The gift of celibacy is the special ability that God gives to certain members of the Body of Christ to remain single and enjoy it; to be unmarried and not suffer undue sexual temptations.
Matthew 19:10-12 - 1 Corinthians 7:7,8

W. Intercession. The gift of intercession is the special ability that God gives to certain members of the Body of Christ to pray for extended periods of time on a regular basis and see frequent and specific answers to their prayers, to a degree much greater than that which is expected of the average Christian.
Luke 22:41-44 - Acts 12:12 - Colossians 1:9-12 - Colossians 4:12,13 – 1 Timothy 2:1,2 - James 5:14-16

X. Exorcism. The gift of exorcism is the special ability that God gives to certain members of the Body of Christ to cast out demons and evil spirits.
Matthew 12:22-32 - Luke 10:12-20 - Acts 8:5-8 - Acts 16:16-18

Y. Service. The gift of service is the special ability that God gives to certain members of the Body of Christ to identify the unmet needs involved in a task related to God's work, and to make use of available resources to meet those needs and help accomplish the desired results.
Acts 6:1-7 - Romans 12:7 - Galatians 6:2,10 - 2 Tim. 1:16-18 - Titus 3:14

ROWS	GIFT
A	PROPHECY
B	PASTORING
C	TEACHING
D	WISDOM
E	KNOWLEDGE
F	EXHORTATION
G	DISCERNING
H	GIVING
I	HELPS
J	MERCY
K	MISSIONARY
L	EVANGELIST
M	HOSPITALITY
N	FAITH
O	LEADERSHIP
P	ADMINISTRATION
Q	MIRACLES

ROWS	GIFT
R	HEALING
S	TONGUES
T	INTERPRETATION
U	POVERTY
V	CELIBACY
W	INTERCESSION
X	EXORCISM
Y	SERVICE

Other books available from Solomon Osoko:

FATHERHOOD:
Role Modelling God on Earth

Anyone can be a dad, but it takes a real man to be a father. The influence of a father in a child's development surpasses almost every other influence in this world. Being physically present, however, isn't enough to be a good father.
Pastor Solomon Osoko says in this book that:
A father's main purpose is to role model God to his children. The scary question is, "If you are not connected to your Heavenly Father, how can you role model Him effectively on earth?"
How can you give a fatherly love that you do not have to your children? A godly father makes having a relationship with God very easy for his children.
Paperback 160 pages / ISBN **978-3-9524512-1-2**

ART OF TRIUMPHANT PRAYER
Power of Prevailing Prayer

You can become all you want to be if all your prayers are answered. That is why it is very important for you to learn and master the triumphant art of prevailing prayers. "After you learn what the disciples learnt from Jesus Christ about prayer, attending Church prayer meeting will become one of the most exciting activities you will cherish in your Christian walk."
Paperback 120 pages / ISBN 978-3-9523844-2-8

KINGDOM LEADERSHIP
Serving Your Generation

Leadership is an all time important topic to mankind. Many homes, businesses and countries have been ruined for bad leadership. Because leadership problem concerns all men, different institutions have sought different solutions to it. I have over the years watched how business schools take a business approach; and how political schools take a political approach and how Church institutions take a spiritual approach - all to the same issue. The fact, however, is that each of the approaches, though relevant, is as limited as its purview. There is a need for a bigger view. It all starts with changing the way we see and operate leadership.

Paperback 230 pages / ISBN 978-3-9523844-6-6

FAITHFULNESS IN LEADERSHIP
Discovering fruitfulness in Faithfulness

The rise and fall of every organization depend on its leadership.

Smite the shepherd, and the sheep will scatter!

There is no place where this truth is more relevant than in the Church of Christ where it requires the united efforts of a mature congregation and faithful leadership to fulfil God's purpose for His Church. Only rooted and well-established people can bear fruits. Only a faithful leadership, conscious of its responsibility and focused on its calling can take its organization to the next level. We need a culture of faithfulness to reap fruits of our labour. Remember that a big oak tree was once a tiny seed that refused to give up.

Only finishers can be winners.

Paperback 160 pages / ISBN 978-3-9523844-5-9

GLOWING FROM GLORY TO GLORY
366 Days Devotional

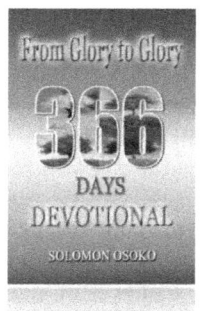

Successful walk with the Lord begins with a changed heart, perception and action.
Let Pastor Solomon Osoko lead you on a path of transformation that will take you to a sure destination of joy, perfection and fulfilment. Allow the rich revelations of the word of God in this book to set you aglow from glory to glory. Rise up and shine!
Paperback 370 pages / ISBN 978-3-9523844-9-7

FELLOWSHIP
The power link to dominion

Fellowship with man has always remained a goal of high importance to God from the beginning of creation. For that reason, He made provision for fellowship with every man to be possible.
In this book,
Pastor Solomon Osoko boldly affirms that:
"Every form of evil is a departure from the good plan of God and is perpetuated where fellowship with God is dishonoured or broken. Every man living outside of fellowship with his Maker simply makes self a defenceless prey for the enemy."
Paperback 210 pages / ISBN 978-3-9523844-1-1

FULFILLING YOUR DESTINY

Living a fulfilled and impactful life

There is no gain, but chain for a born again Christian that will not use his brain. No matter how born again you are, if you refuse to use your brain, you will fail again. This book will go beyond helping you to locate and fulfil your destiny to establishing your feet on the part of divine fulfilment. You will also discover:
- 4 steps to fulfilling your destiny
- 5 steps to fulfilling your divine purpose
- 6 stages of life
- 12 kingdom keys to keep your heaven open

Paperback 204 pages / ISBN: 978-9523094-0-7

GOD'S KEY TO SUPERNATURAL BLESSING:

Sowing a soaring seed.

This book is particularly dedicated to destroying clouds of ignorance the enemy has been using over the years to cut off the children of the Lord from their heavenly provision and protection thereby subjecting them to sickness, abject poverty, failures and curses.
In this book, you will discover:

- the seven seed principles
- the seven harvest principles
- the impartiality of divine blessing
- all you need to know about tithing

Paperback 192 pages / ISBN: 978-9523094-1-4

BORN AGAIN TO WIN
Taking a full step of faith

This powerful book, spiced with practical faith exercise at the end of every chapter, is sure to help you take the full step of faith in to your covenant inheritance in God.

Paperback 120 pages / ISBN 978-3-9523844-0-4

40 RELECTIONS ON RELATIONSHIP

What makes a difference between a recluse and a regent? Attitude to relationship!
Building a great relationship is a major responsibility of every decent citizen of the world who aspires to enjoy peace, love and unity in his or her world.
In this book, Ps Solomon Osoko says:
"There is no second opportunity to make the first impression. Mastering good human relationship can easily open you up to your wealthy realms. There is nothing you lack that is not available in other people around you. All you need is the finesse to freely unlock such resources and permit them to enrich your life and that of many others that are connected to you."

In this book, you will learn reasons, rules and revelations on building a rational relationship.

Paperback 115 pages / ISBN: 978-3-9523844-8-0

You are lovingly invited to
FELLOWSHIP with us
@ Christ International Church

Baden: Mellingerstrase 26, 5400 Baden, Switzerland
Bern: Waldeggstr.37, 3097 Liebefeld – Bern (Koniz), Switzerland
www.cichurch.org
info@cichurch.org

***

Also visit our Bible School:
@ Christ International Bible School

For more information:
www.cibsworld.org
info@cibsworld.org

www.ingramcontent.com/pod-product-compliance
Lightning Source LLC
Chambersburg PA
CBHW031405160426
43196CB00007B/907